THE CHRONICLES OF CANADA

THIRTY-TWO VOLUMES ILLUSTRATED

Edited by GEORGE M. WRONG and H. H. LANGTON

THE CHRONICLES OF CANADA

THE CHRONICLES OF CANADA

THE CHRONICLES OF CANADA

TORONTO: GLASGOW, BROOK & COMPANY

THE FATHERS OF
CONFEDERATION

BY

A. H. U. COLQUHOUN

THE FATHERS OF CONFEDERATION

After the painting by Robert Harris

THE FATHERS OF CONFEDERATION

A Chronicle of the Birth of
the Dominion

BY

A. H. U. COLQUHOUN

EX UNO
DISCE OMNES

TORONTO
GLASGOW, BROOK & COMPANY
1916

TO

COLONEL GEORGE T. DENISON

WHOSE LIFE-WORK IS PROOF THAT
LOYALTY TO THE EMPIRE IS
FIDELITY TO CANADA

CONTENTS

ILLUSTRATIONS

CHAPTER I

THE DAWN OF THE MOVEMENT

THE sources of the Canadian Dominion must be sought in the period immediately following the American Revolution. In 1783 the Treaty of Paris granted independence to the Thirteen Colonies. Their vast territories, rich resources, and hardy population were lost to the British crown. From the ruins of the Empire, so it seemed for the moment, the young Republic rose. The issue of the struggle gave no indication that British power in America could ever be revived ; and King George mournfully hoped that posterity would not lay at his door ' the downfall of this once respectable empire.'

But, disastrous as the war had proved, there still remained the fragments of the once mighty domain. If the treaty of peace had shorn the Empire of the Thirteen Colonies and the great region south of the Lakes, it had left unimpaired the provinces to the east and north — Nova Scotia, Newfoundland, and Canada—while still farther north and west an unexplored continent in itself, stretching to the Pacific Ocean, was either held in the tight grip of the Hudson's Bay Company or was shortly to be won by its intrepid rival, the North-West Company of Montreal. There were not lacking men of prescience and courage who looked beyond the misfortunes of the hour, and who saw in the dominions still vested in the crown an opportunity to repair the shattered empire and restore it to a modified splendour. A general union of the colonies had been mooted before the Revolution. The idea naturally cropped up again as a means of consolidating what was left. Those who on the king's side had borne a leading part in the conflict took to heart the lesson it conveyed. Foremost among these were Lord Dorchester, whom Canada had long known as Guy Carleton, and William Smith, the Loyalist refugee from New York, who was appointed chief justice of Lower Canada. Each had special claims to be consulted on the future government of the country. During the war Dorchester's military services in preserving Canada from the invaders had been of supreme value ; and his occupation

of New York after the peace, while he guided
and protected the Loyalist emigration, had
furnished a signal proof of his vigour and
sagacity. William Smith belonged to a
family of distinction in the old colony of New
York. He possessed learning and probity.
His devotion to the crown had cost him his
fortune. It appears that it was with him,
rather than with Dorchester, that the plan
originated of uniting the British provinces
under a central government. The two were
close friends and had gone to England together.
They came out to Quebec in company, the one
as governor-general, the other as chief justice.
The period of confusion, when constructive
measures were on foot, suggested to them the
need of some general authority which would
ensure unity of administration.

And so, in October 1789, when Grenville,
the secretary of state, sent to Dorchester the
draft of the measure passed in 1791 to divide
Quebec into Upper and Lower Canada, and
invited such observations as ' experience and
local knowledge may suggest,' Dorchester
wrote :

I have to submit to the wisdom of His
Majesty's councils, whether it may not be

advisable to establish a general government for His Majesty's dominions upon
this continent, as well as a governor-
general, whereby the united exertions of
His Majesty's North American Provinces
may more effectually be directed to the
general interest and to the preservation of
the unity of the Empire. I inclose a copy
of a letter from the Chief Justice, with
some additional clauses upon this subject
prepared by him at my request.

The letter referred to made a plea for a comprehensive plan bringing all the provinces together, rather than a scheme to perpetuate
local divisions. It reflected the hopes of the
Loyalists then and of their descendants at a
later day. In William Smith's view it was
an imperfect system of government, not the
policy of the mother country, that had brought
on the Revolution. There are few historical
documents relating to Canada which possess
as much human interest as the reminiscent
letter of the old chief justice, with its melan-
choly recital of former mistakes, its reminder
that Britons going beyond the seas would inevitably carry with them their instinct for
liberal government, and its striking prophecy

WILLIAM SMITH
From a portrait in the Parliament Buildings, Ottawa

that ' the new nation ' about to be created
would prove a source of strength to Great
Britain. Many a year was to elapse before
the prophecy should come true. This was
due less to the indifference of statesmen than
to the inherent difficulties of devising a workable plan. William Smith's idea of confederation was a central legislative body, in addition
to the provincial legislatures, this legislative
body to consist of a council nominated by the
crown and of a general assembly. The
members of the assembly were to be chosen
by the elective branches of the provincial
legislatures. No law should be effective until
it passed in the assembly ' by such and so
many voices as will make it the Act of the
majority of the Provinces.' The central body
must meet at least once every two years, and
could sit for seven years unless sooner dissolved. There were provisions for maintaining the authority of the crown and the Imperial parliament over all legislation. The
bill, however, made no attempt to limit the
powers of the local legislatures and to reserve
certain subjects to the general assembly. It
would have brought forth, as drafted, but a
crude instrument of government. The outline of the measure revealed the honest en-

thusiasm of the Loyalists for unity, but as a constitution for half a continent, remote and unsettled, it was too slight in texture and would have certainly broken down. Grenville replied at length to Dorchester's other suggestions, but of the proposed general parliament he wrote this only : ' The formation of a general legislative government for all the King's provinces in America is a point which has been under consideration, but I think it liable to considerable objection.'

Thus briefly was the first definite proposal set aside. The idea, however, had taken root and never ceased to show signs of life. As time wore on, the provincial constitutions proved unsatisfactory. At each outbreak of political agitation and discontent, in one quarter or another, some one was sure to come forward with a fresh plea for intercolonial union. Nor did the entreaty always emanate from men of pronounced Loyalist convictions; it sometimes came from root-and-branch Reformers like Robert Gourlay and William Lyon Mackenzie.

The War of 1812 furnished another startling proof of the isolated and defenceless position of the provinces. The relations between Upper Canada and Lower Canada, never cordial, became worse. In 1814, at the close of the war, Chief Justice Sewell of Quebec, in a correspondence with the Duke of Kent (Queen Victoria's father), disclosed a plan for a small central parliament of thirty members with subordinate legislatures.[1] Sewell was a son-in-law of Chief Justice Smith and shared his views. The duke suggested that these legislatures need be only two in number, because the Canadas should be reunited and the three Atlantic colonies placed under one government. No one heeded the suggestion. A few years intervened, and an effort was made to patch up a satisfactory arrangement between Lower Canada and Upper Canada. The two provinces quarrelled over the division of the customs revenue. When the dispute had reached a critical stage a bill was introduced in the Imperial parliament to unite them. This was in 1822. But the proposal to force two disputing neighbours to dwell together in the same house as a remedy for disagreements failed to evoke enthusiasm from either. The friends of federation then drew together, and Sewell joined hands with Bishop Strachan

[1] It has been said that Attorney-General Uniacke of Nova Scotia submitted, in 1809, a measure for a general union, but of this there does not appear to be any authentic record.

and John Beverley Robinson of Upper Canada in reviving the plea for a wider union and in placing the arguments in its favour before the Imperial government.   Brenton Halliburton, judge of the Supreme Court of Nova Scotia (afterwards chief justice), wrote a pamphlet to help on the cause.   The Canada union bill fell through, the revenue dispute being settled on another basis, but the discussion of federation proceeded.

To this period belongs the support given to the project by William Lyon Mackenzie. Writing in 1824 to Mr Canning, he believed that

a union of all the colonies, with a government suitably poised and modelled, so as to have under its eye the resources of our whole territory and having the means in its power to administer impartial justice in all its bounds, to no one part at the expense of another, would require few boons from Britain, and would advance her interests much more in a few years than the bare right of possession of a barren, uncultivated wilderness of lake and forest, with some three or four inhabitants to the square mile, can do in centuries.

Here we have the whole picture drawn in a few strokes. Mackenzie had vision and brilliancy. If he had given himself wholly to this task, posterity would have passed a verdict upon his career different from that now accepted. As late as in 1833 he declared : ' I have long desired to see a conference assembled at Quebec, consisting of delegates freely elected by the people of the six northern colonies, to express to England the opinion of the whole body on matters of great general interest.' But instead of pursuing this idea he threw himself into the mad project of armed rebellion, and the fruits of that folly were unfavourable for a long time to the dreams of federation. Lord Durham came. He found ' the leading minds of the various colonies strongly and generally inclined to a scheme that would elevate their countries into something like a national existence.' Such a scheme, he rightly argued, would not weaken the connection with the Empire, and the closing passages of his Report are memorable for the insight and statesmanship with which the solid advantages of union are discussed. If Lord Durham erred, it was in advocating the immediate union of the two Canadas as the first necessary step, and in announcing as one of his objects the assimilation to the prevailing British type in Canada of the French-Canadian race, a thing which, as events proved, was neither possible nor necessary.

Many of the advocates of union, never blessed with much confidence in their cause, were made timid by this point of Durham's reasoning. His arguments, which were intended to urge the advantages of a complete reform in the system and machinery of government, produced for a time a contrary effect. Governments might propose and parliaments might discuss resolutions of an academic kind, while eloquent men with voice and pen sought to rouse the imaginations of the people. But for twenty years after the union of the Canadas in 1841 federation remained little more than a noble aspiration. The statesmen who wielded power looked over the field and sighed that the time had not yet come.

CHAPTER II

OBSTACLES TO UNION

THE prospect was indeed one to dismay the most ardent patriot. After the passage of the Constitutional Act of 1791 the trend of events had set steadily in the direction of separation. Nature had placed physical obstacles in the road to union, and man did his best to render the task of overcoming them as hopeless as possible. The land communication between the Maritime Provinces and Canada, such as it was, precluded effective intercourse. In winter there could be no access by the St Lawrence, so that Canada's winter port was in the United States. As late as 1850 it took ten days, often longer, for a letter to go from Halifax to Toronto. Previous to 1867 there were but two telegraph lines connecting Halifax with Canada. Messages by wire were a luxury, the rate between Quebec and Toronto being seventy-five cents for ten words and eight cents for each additional word. Neither commerce nor friendship could be much developed by telegraph in those days, and, as the rates were based on the distance, a telegram sent from Upper Canada to Nova Scotia was a costly affair. To reach the Red River Settlement, the nucleus of Manitoba, the Canadian travelled through the United States. With the colonies of Vancouver Island and British Columbia the East had practically no dealings. Down to 1863, as Sir Richard Cartwright once said,[1] there existed for the average Canadian no North-West. A great lone land there was, and a few men in parliament looked forward to its ultimate acquisition, but popular opinion regarded it vaguely as something dim and distant. In course of time railways came, but they were not interprovincial and they did nothing to bind the East to the West. The railway service of early days is not to be confounded with the rapid trains of to-day, when a traveller leaves Montreal after ten in the morning and finds himself in Toronto before six o'clock in the afternoon. Said Cartwright, in the address already cited :

Even in our own territory, and it was a matter not to be disregarded, the state

[1] Address to Canadian Club, Ottawa, 1906.

of communication was exceedingly slow
and imperfect. Practically the city of
Quebec was almost as far from Toronto in
those days, during a great part of the year,
as Ottawa is from Vancouver to-day. I
can remember, myself, on one occasion
being on a train which took four days to
make its way from Prescott to Ottawa.

Each province had its own constitution, its
tariff, postage laws, and currency. It promoted its own interests, regardless of the existence of its British neighbours. Differences
arose, says one writer, between their codes of
law, their public institutions, and their commercial regulations.[1] Provincial misunder-
standings, that should have been avoided,
seriously retarded the building of the Intercolonial Railway. ' The very currencies differ,'
said Lord Carnarvon in the House of Lords.
' In Canada the pound or the dollar are legal
tender. In Nova Scotia, the Peruvian, Mexican, Columbian dollars are all legal ; in New
Brunswick, British and American coins are
recognized by law, though I believe that the
shilling is taken at twenty-four cents, which
is less than its value ; in Newfoundland, Peru-

[1] *Union of the Colonies,* by P. S. Hamilton.   Halifax, 1864.

vian, Mexican, Columbian, old Spanish dollars, are all equally legal ; whilst in Prince Edward's Island the complexity of currencies and of their relative value is even greater.' When the Reciprocity Treaty was negotiated at Washington in 1854, Nova Scotia felt, with some reason, that she had not been adequately consulted in the granting to foreign fishermen of her inshore fisheries. In a word, the chief political forces were centrifugal, not centripetal. All the jealousy, the factious spirit, and the prejudice, which petty local sovereignties are bound to engender, flourished apace; and the general effect was to develop what European statesmen of a certain period termed Particularism. The marvel is not that federation lagged, but that men with vision and courage, forced to view these depressing conditions at close range, were able to keep the idea alive.

There was some advance in public opinion between 1850 and 1860, but, on the whole, adverse influences prevailed and little was achieved. The effects of separate political development and of divided interest were deeply rooted. Leaders of opinion in the various provinces, and even men of the same province, refused to join hands for any great national purpose. Party conflict absorbed their best energies. To this period, however, belongs the spadework which laid the foundations of the future structure. The British American League held its various meetings and adopted its resolutions. But the League was mainly a party counterblast to the Annexation Manifesto of 1849 and soon disappeared. To this period, too, belong the writings of able advocates of union like P. S. Hamilton of Halifax and J. C. Taché of Quebec, whose treatises possess even to-day more than historical value. Another notable contribution to the subject was the lecture by Alexander Morris entitled *Nova Britannia*, first delivered at Montreal in 1858 and afterwards published. Yet such propaganda aroused no perceptible enthusiasm. In Great Britain the whole question of colonial relations was in process of evolution, while her statesmen were doubtful, as ours were, of what the ultimate end would be. That a full conception of colonial self-government had not yet dawned is shown by these words, written in 1852 by Earl Grey to Lord John Russell : ' *It is obvious that if the colonies are not to become independent states, some kind of authority must be exercised by the Government at home.*'

This decade, however, witnessed some de-

finite political action.   In 1854 Johnston, the
Conservative Opposition leader in the Nova
Scotia legislature, presented a motion in these
terms : ' *Resolved*, That the union or confederation of the British Provinces on just
principles, while calculated to perpetuate their
connection with the parent state, will promote
their advancement, increase their strength and
influence, and elevate their position.'   This
resolution, academic in form, but supported in
a well-balanced and powerful speech by the
mover, drew from Joseph Howe, then leader
of the government, his preference for representation in the British House of Commons.
The attitude of Howe, then and afterwards,
should be examined with impartiality, because
he and other British Americans, as well as
some English statesmen, were the victims of
the honest doubts which command respect
but block the way to action.   Johnston, as
prime minister in 1857, pressed his policy upon
the Imperial government, but met with no
response.   When Howe returned to power, he
carried a motion which declared for a conference to promote either the union of the Maritime Provinces or a general federation, but
expressing no preference for either.   Howe
never was pledged to federation as his fixed

SIR ALEXANDER T. GALT

From a photograph by Topley

policy, as so many persons have asserted. He made various declarations which betokened uncertainty. So little had the efforts put forth down to 1861 impressed the official mind that Lord Mulgrave, the governor of Nova Scotia, in forwarding Howe's motion to the Colonial Office, wrote : ' As an abstract question the union of the North American colonies has long received the support of many persons of weight and ability, but so far as I am aware, no political mode of carrying out this union has ever been proposed.'

The most encouraging step taken at this time, and the most far-reaching in its consequences, was the action of Alexander Galt in Canada. Galt possessed a strong and independent mind. The youngest son of John Galt, the Scottish novelist, he had come across the ocean in the service of the British American Land Company, and had settled at Sherbrooke in the Eastern Townships of Lower Canada. Though personally influential and respected, he wielded no general political authority, for he lacked the aptitude for compromise demanded in the game of party. He was the outspoken champion of Protestant interests in the Catholic part of Canada, and had boldly declared for the annexation of Canada to the

United States in the agitation of 1849.   His
views on clericalism he never greatly modified,
but annexation to the United States he aban-
doned, with characteristic candour, for federation.   In 1858 he advocated a federal union
of all the provinces in a telling speech in parliament, which revealed a thorough knowledge
of the material resources of the country, afterwards issued in book form in his *Canada :
1849 to 1859*.   During the ministerial crisis of
August 1858 Sir Edmund Head asked Galt to
form a government.   He declined, and indicated George Cartier as a fit and proper person
to do so.   The former Conservative Cabinet,
with some changes, then resumed office, and
Galt himself, exacting a pledge that Confederation should form part of the government's
policy, assumed the portfolio of Finance.   The
pledge was kept in the speech of the governor-
general closing the session, and in October of
that year Cartier, with two of his colleagues,
Galt and Ross, visited London to secure approval for a meeting of provincial delegates
on union.   Galt's course had forced the question out of the sphere of speculation.   A careful student of the period [1] argues with point

[1] See the chapter, 'Parties and Politics, 1840-1867,' by J. L.
Morison, in *Canada and its Provinces*, vol. v.

that to Galt we owe the introduction of the
policy into practical politics. In the light of
after events this view cannot be lightly set
aside. But the effort bore no fruit for the
moment. The colonial secretary, Sir Edward
Bulwer Lytton, declined to authorize the
conference without first consulting the other
provinces, and the government did not feel
itself bound because of this to resign or consult the constituencies. In other words, the
question did not involve the fate of the Cabinet.
But Galt had gained a great advantage. He
had enlisted the support of Cartier, whose
influence in Lower Canada was henceforth
exerted with fidelity to win over the French
to a policy which they had long resisted. The
cause attained additional strength in 1860 by
the action of two other statesmen, George
Brown and John A. Macdonald, who between
them commanded the confidence of Upper
Canada, the one as Liberal, the other as Conservative leader. Brown brought before parliament resolutions embodying the decisions of
the Reform Convention of 1859 in favour of a
federation confined to the Canadas, and Macdonald declared unequivocally for federative
union as a principle, arguing that a strong
central government should be the chief aim.

Brown's resolutions were rejected, and the movement so auspiciously begun once more exhibited an ominous tendency to subside. The varying fortunes which attended the cause during these years resembled its previous vicissitudes. It appeared as if all were for a party and none were for the state. If those who witnessed the events of 1860 had been asked for their opinion, they would probably have declared that the problem was as far from solution as ever. Yet they would have been mistaken, as the near future was to show. A great war was close at hand, and, as war so often does, it stimulated movements and policies which otherwise might have lain dormant. The situation which arose out of the Civil War in the United States neither created nor carried Confederation, but it resulted, through a sense of common danger, in bringing the British provinces together and in giving full play to all the forces that were making for their union.

CHAPTER III

THE EVE OF CONFEDERATION

A DAY of loftier ideas and greater issues in all the provinces was about to dawn. The ablest politicians had been prone to wrangle like washerwomen over a tub, colouring the parliamentary debates by personal rivalry and narrow aims, while measures of first-rate importance went unheeded. The change did not occur in the twinkling of an eye, for the cherished habits of two generations were not to be discarded so quickly. Goldwin Smith asserted [1] that, whoever laid claim to the parentage of Confederation, the real parent was Deadlock. But this was the critic, not the historian, who spoke. The causes lay far deeper than in the breakdown of party government in Canada. Events of profound significance were about to change an atmosphere overladen with partisanship and to strike the imaginations of men.

[1] *Canada and the Canadian Question,* by Goldwin Smith, p. 143.

The first factor in the national awakening was the call of the great western domain. British Americans began to realize that they were the heirs of a rich and noble possession. The idea was not entirely new. The fur traders had indeed long tried to keep secret the truth as to the fertility of the plains ; but men who had been born or had lived in the West were now settled in the East. They had stories to tell, and their testimony was emphatic. In 1856 the Imperial authorities had intimated to Canada that, as the licence of the Hudson's Bay Company to an exclusive trade in certain regions would expire in 1859, it was intended to appoint a select committee of the British House of Commons to investigate the existing situation in those territories and to report upon their future status; and Canada had sent Chief Justice Draper to London as her commissioner to watch the proceedings, to give evidence, and to submit to his government any proposals that might be made. Simultaneously a select committee of the Canadian Assembly sat to hear evidence and to report a basis for legislation. Canada boldly claimed that her western boundary was the Pacific ocean, and this prospect had long encouraged men like George Brown to look forward to extension westward, and to advocate it, as one solution of Upper Canada's political grievances. It was a vision calculated to rouse the adventurous spirit of the British race in colonizing and in developing vast and unknown lands. Another wonderful page was about to open in the history of British expansion. And, hand in hand with romance, went the desire for dominion and commerce.

But if the call of the West drew men partly by its material attractions, another event, of a wholly different sort, appealed vividly to their sentiment. In 1860 the young Prince of Wales visited the provinces as the representative of his mother, the beloved Queen Victoria. His tour resembled a triumphal progress. It evoked feelings and revived memories which the young prince himself, pleasing though his personality was, could not have done. It was the first clear revelation of the intensity of that attachment to the traditions and institutions of the Empire which in our own day has so vitally affected the relations of the self-governing states to the mother country. In a letter from Ottawa [1] to Lord Palmerston,

[1] *Life of Henry Pelham, fifth Duke of Newcastle,* by John Martineau, p. 292.

the Duke of Newcastle, the prince's tutor, wrote :

> I never saw in any part of England such extensive or beautiful outward demonstrations of respect and affection, either to the Queen or to any private object of local interest, as I have seen in every one of these colonies, and, what is more important, there have been circumstances attending all these displays which have marked their sincerity and proved that neither curiosity nor self-interest were the only or the ruling influences.

Of all the events, however, that startled the British provinces out of the self-absorbed contemplation of their own little affairs, the Civil War in the United States exerted the most immediate influence. It not only brought close the menace of a war between Great Britain and the Republic, with Canada as the battle-ground, but it forced a complete readjustment of our commercial relations. Not less important, the attitude of the Imperial government toward Confederation underwent a change. It was D'Arcy McGee who perceived, at the very outset, the probable bearing of the Civil War upon the future of Canada. 'I said in the House during the session of 1861,' he subsequently declared, ' that the first gun fired at Fort Sumter had a message for us.' The situation became plainer when the *Trent* Affair embroiled Great Britain directly with the North, and the safety of Canada appeared to be threatened. While Lincoln was anxiously pondering the British demand that the Confederate agents, Mason and Slidell, removed by an American warship from the British steamer the *Trent*, should be given up, and Lord Lyons was labouring to preserve peace, the fate of Canada hung in the balance. The agents were released, but there followed ten years of unfriendly relations between Great Britain and the United States. There were murmurs that when the South was subdued the trained armies of the North would be turned against the British provinces. The termination of the Reciprocity Treaty, which provided for a large measure of free trade between the two countries, was seen to be reasonably sure. The treaty had existed through a period which favoured a large increase in the exports of the provinces. The Crimean War at first and the Civil War later had created an unparalleled demand for the food products which Canada could supply; and although the records showed the enhanced trade to be mutually profitable, with a balance rather in favour of the United States, the anti-British feeling in the Republic was directed against the treaty. Thus military defence and the necessity of finding new markets became two pressing problems for Canada.

From the Imperial authorities there came now at last distinct encouragement. Hitherto they had hung back. The era of economic dogma in regard to free trade, to some minds more authoritative than Holy Writ, was at its height. Even Cobden was censured because, in the French treaty of 1861, he had departed from the free trade theory. The doctrine of *laissez-faire*, carried to extremes, meant that the colonies should be allowed to cut adrift. But the practical English mind saw the sense and statesmanship of a British American union, and the tone of the colonial secretary changed. In July 1862 the Duke of Newcastle, who then held that office and who did not share the indifference of so many of his predecessors[1] to the colonial connection, wrote sympathetically to Lord Mulgrave, the governor of Nova Scotia:

[1] Between 1852 and 1870 there were thirteen colonial secretaries.

If a union, either partial or complete, should hereafter be proposed with the concurrence of all the Provinces to be united, I am sure that the matter would be weighed in this country both by the public, by Parliament, and by Her Majesty's Government, with no other feeling than an anxiety to discern and promote any course which might be the most conducive to the prosperity, the strength and the harmony of all the British communities in North America.

Nova Scotia, always to the front on the question, had declared for either a general union or a union of the Maritime Provinces, and this had drawn the dispatch of the Duke of Newcastle. A copy of this dispatch was sent to Lord Monck, the governor-general of Canada, for his information and guidance, so that the attitude of the Imperial authorities was generally known. It remained for the various provincial Cabinets to confer and to arrange a course of action. The omens pointed to union in the near future. But, as it happened, a new Canadian ministry, that of Sandfield Macdonald, had shortly before assumed office, and its members were in no wise pledged to the union project. In fact, as was proved later, several of them, notably the prime minister himself, with Dorion, Holton, and Huntington, regarded federation with suspicion and were its consistent opponents until the final accomplishment.

The negotiations for the joint construction of an intercolonial railway had been proceeding for some time. These the ministry continued, but without enthusiasm. The building of this line had been ardently promoted for years. It was the necessary link to bind the provinces together. To secure Imperial financial aid in one form or another delegates had more than once gone to London. The Duke of Newcastle had announced in April 1862 that the nature and extent of the guarantee which Her Majesty's government would recommend to parliament depended upon the arrangements which the provinces themselves had to propose.[1] There was a conference in Quebec. From Nova Scotia came Howe and Annand, who two years later fought Confederation ; from New Brunswick came Tilley and Peter Mitchell, who carried the cause to victory in their province. Delegates from the Quebec meeting

[1] Dispatch of the colonial secretary to the lieutenant-governor of New Brunswick.

went to London, but the railway plan broke down, and the failure was due to Canada. The episode left a bad impression in the minds of the maritime statesmen, and during the whole of 1863 it seemed as if union were indefinitely postponed. Yet this was the very eve of Confederation, and forces already in motion made it inevitable.

CHAPTER IV

THE HOUR AND THE MEN

THE acceptance of federation in the province of Canada came about with dramatic simplicity. Political deadlock was the occasion, rather than the cause, of this acceptance. Racial and religious differences had bred strife and disunion, but no principle of any substance divided the parties. The absence of large issues had encouraged a senseless rivalry between individuals. Surveying the scene not long after, Goldwin Smith, fresh from English conditions, cynically quoted the proverb : ' the smaller the pit, the fiercer the rats.' The upper and lower branches of parliament were elective, and in both bodies the ablest men in the country held seats. In those days commerce, manufacturing, or banking did not, as they do now, withhold men of marked talent from public affairs. But personal antipathies, magnified into feuds, embittered the relations of men who naturally held many views in

common, and distracted the politics of a province which needed nothing so much as peace
and unity of action.

The central figures in this storm of contro-
versy were George Brown and John A. Macdonald, easily the first personages in their respective parties. The two were antipathetic.
Their dispositions were as wide asunder as the
poles. Brown was serious, bold, and master-
ful. Macdonald concealed unrivalled powers
in statecraft and in the leadership of men
behind a droll humour and convivial habits.
From the first they had been political anta-
gonists. But the differences were more than
political. Neither liked nor trusted the other.
Brown bore a grudge for past attacks reflect-
ing upon his integrity, while Macdonald, despite
his experience in the warfare of party, must
often have winced at the epithets of the *Globe*,
Brown's newspaper. During ten years they
were not on speaking terms. But when they
joined to effect a great object, dear to both,
a truce was declared. ' We acted together,'
wrote Macdonald long after of Brown, ' dined
in public places together, played euchre in
crossing the Atlantic and went into society
in England together. And yet on the day
after he resigned we resumed our old positions

and ceased to speak.' [1] To imagine that of all men those two should combine to carry federation seemed the wildest and most improbable dream. Yet that is what actually happened.

In June 1864, during the session of parliament in Quebec, government by party collapsed. In the previous three years there had been two general elections, and four Cabinets had gone to pieces. And while the politicians wrangled, the popular mind, swayed by influences stronger than party interest, convinced itself that the remedy lay in the federal system. Brown felt that Upper Canada looked to him for relief ; and as early as in 1862 he had conveyed private intimation to his Conservative opponents that if they would ensure Upper Canada's just preponderance in parliamentary representation, which at that date the Liberal ministry of Sandfield Macdonald refused to do, they would receive his countenance and approval. In 1864 he moved for a select committee of nineteen members to consider the prospects of federal union. It sat with closed doors. A few hours before the defeat of the Taché-Macdonald ministry in

[1] *Memoirs of Sir John Macdonald,* by Sir Joseph Pope, vol. i, p. 265.

GEORGE BROWN

From a photograph in the possession of Mrs Freeland Barbour,
Edinburgh

June, he, the chairman of the committee, reported to the House that

> a strong feeling was found to exist among the members of the committee in favour of changes in the direction of a federative system, applied either to Canada alone, or to the whole British North American provinces, and such progress has been made as to warrant the committee in recommending that the subject be referred to a committee at the next session of Parliament.

Three years later, on the first Dominion Day, the *Globe*,[1] in discussing this committee and its work, declared that ' a very free interchange of opinion took place. In the course of the discussions it appeared probable that a union of parties might be effected for the purpose of grappling with the constitutional difficulties.' Macdonald voted against the committee's report. Brown was thoroughly in earnest, and the desperate nature of the political situation gave him an opportunity to prove his sincerity and his unselfishness.

[1] This portion of the lengthy survey of the new Dominion in the *Globe* of July 1, 1867, is said to have been written by George Brown himself.

On the evening of Tuesday, June 14, 1864, immediately after the defeat of the ministry on an unimportant question, Brown spoke to two Conservative members and promised to co-operate with any government that would settle the constitutional difficulty. These members, Alexander Morris and John Henry Pope, were on friendly terms with him and became serviceable intermediaries. They were asked to communicate this promise to Macdonald and to Galt. The next day saw the reconciliation of the two leaders who had been estranged for ten years. They met ' standing in the centre of the Assembly Room ' (the formal memorandum is meticulously exact in these and other particulars), that is, neither member crossing to that side of the House led by the other. Macdonald spoke first, mentioning the overtures made and asking if Brown had any ' objection ' to meet Galt and himself. Brown replied, ' Certainly not.' Morris arranged an interview, and the following day Macdonald and Galt called upon Brown at the St Louis Hotel, Quebec. Negotiations, ending in the famous coalition, began.

The memorandum read to the House re-lated in detail every step taken to bring about the coalition, from the opening conversation

which Brown had with Morris and Pope. It
was proper that a full explanation should be
given to the public of a political event so extra-
ordinary and so unexpected. But the narrative of minute particulars indicates the complete lack of confidence existing between the
parties to the agreement. The relationships
of social life rest upon the belief that there is a
code of honour, affecting words and actions,
which is binding upon gentlemen. The memorandum appeared to assume that in political
life these considerations did not exist, and
that unless the whole of the proceedings were
set forth in chronological order, and with am-
plitude of detail, some of the group would
seek to repudiate the explanation on one point
or another, while the general public would dis-
believe them all. To such a pass had the
extremes of partyism brought the leading men
in parliament. If, however, the memorandum
is a very human document, it is also histori-
cally most interesting and important. The
leaders began by solemnly assuring each other
that nothing but ' the extreme urgency of the
present crisis ' could justify their meeting together for common political action. The idea
that the paramount interests of the nation,
threatened by possible invasion and by com-

mercial disturbance, would be ground for such a junction of forces does not seem to have suggested itself. After the preliminary skirmishing upon matters of party concern the negotiators at last settled down to business.

Mr Brown asked what the Government proposed as a remedy for the injustice complained of by Upper Canada, and as a settlement of the sectional trouble. Mr Macdonald and Mr Galt replied that their remedy was a Federal Union of all the British North American Provinces; local matters being committed to local bodies, and matters common to all to a General Legislature.[1]

Mr Brown rejoined that this would not be acceptable to the people of Upper Canada as a remedy for existing evils. That he believed that federation of all the provinces ought to come, and would come about ere long, but it had not yet been thoroughly considered by the people; and even were this otherwise, there were

---

[1] Sir Joseph Pope states that in the printed copy of this memorandum which Sir John Macdonald preserved there appears, immediately following the word 'Legislature' at the end of this paragraph, in the handwriting of Mr Brown, these words: 'Constituted on the well-understood principles of federal gov.'

so many parties to be consulted that its
adoption was uncertain and remote.

Mr Brown was then asked what his
remedy was, when he stated that the measure acceptable to Upper Canada would
be Parliamentary Reform, based on population, without regard to a separating
line between Upper and Lower Canada.
To this both Mr Macdonald and Mr Galt
stated that it was impossible for them to
accede, or for any Government to carry
such a measure, and that, unless a basis
could be found on the federation principle
suggested by the report of Mr Brown's committee, it did not appear to them likely
that anything could be settled.

At this stage, then, Brown thought federation should be limited to Canada, believing
the larger scheme uncertain and remote, while
the others preferred a federal union for all the
provinces. At a later meeting Cartier joined
the gathering and a confidential statement
was drawn up (the disinclination to take one
another's word being still a lively sentiment),
so that Brown could consult his friends. The
ministerial promise in its final terms was as
follows :

The Government are prepared to pledge themselves to bring in a measure next session for the purpose of removing existing difficulties by introducing the federal principle into Canada, coupled with such provisions as will permit the Maritime Provinces and the North-West Territory to be incorporated into the same system of government. And the Government will seek, by sending representatives to the Lower Provinces and to England, to secure the assent of those interests which are beyond the control of our own legislation to such a measure as may enable all British North America to be united under a General Legislature based upon the federal principle.

This basis gave satisfaction all round, and the proceedings relapsed into the purely political diplomacy which forms the least pleasant phase of what was otherwise a highly patriotic episode, creditable in its results to all concerned. Brown fought hard for a representation of four Liberals in the Cabinet, preferring to remain out of it himself, and, when his inclusion was deemed indispensable, offering to join as a minister without portfolio or salary.

THE HOUR AND THE MEN 39

Finally Macdonald promised to confer with him upon the personnel of the Conservative element in the Cabinet, so that the incoming Liberals would meet colleagues with whom harmonious relations should be ensured. The fates ordained that, since Brown had been the first to propose the sacrifice of party to country, the arrangement arrived at was the least advantageous to his interests. He had the satisfaction of feeling that the Upper Canada Liberals in the House supported his action, but those from Lower Canada, both English and French, were entirely unsympathetic. The Lower Canada section of the ministry accordingly remained wholly Conservative.

It does not require much depth of political experience to realize the embarrassment of Brown's position. The terms were not easy for him. In a ministry of twelve members he and two colleagues would be the only Liberals. The leadership of Upper Canada, and in fact the real premiership, because Taché was frail and past his prime, would rest with Macdonald. The presidency of the Executive Council, which was offered him, unless joined to the office of prime minister, was of no real importance. Some party friends throughout the country

would misunderstand, and more would scoff.
He had parted company with his loyal personal friends Dorion and Holton. If, as
Disraeli said, England does not love coalitions,
neither does Canada.   For the time being, and,
as events proved, for a considerable time, the
Liberal party would be divided and helpless,
because the pledge of Brown pledged also the
fighting strength of the party.   Although the
union issue dwarfed all others, questions would
arise, awkward questions like that of patronage, old questions with a new face, on which
there had been vehement differences.   For
two of his new colleagues, Macdonald and Galt,
Brown entertained feelings far from cordial.
Cautious advisers like Alexander Mackenzie
and Oliver Mowat counselled against a coalition, suggesting that the party should support
the government, but should not take a share
in it.   All this had to be weighed and a decision reached quickly.   But Brown had put
his hand to the plough and would not turn
back.   With the dash and determination that
distinguished him, he accepted the proposal,
became president of the Executive Council,
with Sir Etienne Taché as prime minister, and
selected William McDougall and Oliver Mowat
as his Liberal colleagues.   Amazement and

consternation ran like wildfire throughout Upper Canada when the news arrived from Quebec that Brown and Macdonald were members of the same government. At the outset Brown had feared that ' the public mind would be shocked,' and he was not wrong. But the sober second thought of the country in both parties applauded the act, and the desire for union found free vent. Posterity has endorsed the course taken by Brown and justly honours his memory for having, at the critical hour and on terms that would have made the ordinary politician quail, rendered Confederation possible. There is evidence that the Conservative members of the coalition played the game fairly and redeemed their promise to put union in the forefront of their policy. On this issue complete concord reigned in the Cabinet. The natural divergences of opinion on minor points in the scheme were arranged without internal discord. This was fortunate, because grave obstacles were soon to be encountered.

If George Brown of Upper Canada was the hero of the hour, George Cartier of Lower Canada played a rôle equally courageous and honourable. The hostile forces to be encountered by the French-Canadian leader were formidable. Able men of his own race, like Dorion, Letellier, and Fournier, prepared to fight tooth and nail. The Rouges, as the Liberals there were termed, opposed him to a man. The idea of British American union had in the past been almost invariably put forward as a means of destroying the influence of the French. Influential representatives, too, of the English minority in Lower Canada, like Dunkin, Holton, and Huntington, opposed it. Joly de Lotbinière, the French Protestant, warned the Catholics and the French that federation would endanger their rights. The Rouge resistance was not a passive parliamentary resistance only, because, later on, the earnest protests of the dissentients were carried to the foot of the throne. But all these influences the intrepid Cartier faced undismayed; and Brown, in announcing his intention to enter the coalition, paid a warm tribute to Cartier for his frank and manly attitude. This was the burial of another hatchet, and the amusing incident related by Cartwright illustrates how it was received.

In that memorable afternoon when Mr Brown, not without emotion, made his

SIR GEORGE CARTIER

From a painting in the Château de Ramezay

statement to a hushed and expectant House, and declared that he was about to ally himself with Sir George Cartier and his friends, for the purpose of carrying out Confederation, I saw an excitable, elderly little French member rush across the floor, climb up on Mr Brown, who, as you remember, was of a stature approaching the gigantic, fling his arms about his neck, and hang several seconds there suspended, to the visible consternation of Mr Brown and to the infinite joy of all beholders, pit, box, and gallery included.

At last statesmanship had taken the place of party bickering, and, as James Ferrier of Montreal, a member of the Legislative Council, remarked in the debates of 1865, the legislators ' all thought, in fact, that a political millennium had arrived.'

CHAPTER V

THE CHARLOTTETOWN CONFERENCE

NOT an instant too soon had unity come in Canada. The coalition ministry, having adjourned parliament, found itself faced with a situation in the Maritime Provinces which called for speedy action.

Nova Scotia, the ancient province by the sea, discouraged by the vacillation of Canada in relation to federation and the construction of the Intercolonial Railway, was bent upon joining forces with New Brunswick and Prince Edward Island. The proposal was in the nature of a reunion, for, when constitutional government had been first set up in Nova Scotia in 1758, the British possessions along the Atlantic coast, save Newfoundland, were all governed as one province from Halifax. But the policy in early days of splitting up the colonies into smaller areas, for convenience of administration, was here faithfully carried out. In 1770 a separate government was conferred

upon Prince Edward Island. In 1784 New
Brunswick was formed. In the same year
the island of Cape Breton was given a governor
and council of its own. Cape Breton was reunited to the parent colony of Nova Scotia in
1820, but three separate provinces remained,
each developing apart from the others, thus
complicating and making more difficult the
whole problem of union when men with fore-
sight and boldness essayed to solve it. Nova
Scotia had kept alive the tradition of leadership. The province which has supplied three
prime ministers to the Canadian Dominion
never lacked statesmen with the imagination to
perceive the advantages which would flow from
the consolidation of British power in America.

In 1864, a few weeks before George Brown
in the Canadian House had moved for his
select committee on federal union, Dr Charles
Tupper proposed, in the legislature of Nova
Scotia, a legislative union of the Maritime
Provinces. The seal of Imperial authority
had been set upon this movement by the dispatch, already quoted, from the Duke of Newcastle to Lord Mulgrave in 1862.

A word concerning the services of Charles
Tupper to the cause of union will be in order
here. None of the Fathers of Confederation

fought a more strenuous battle. None faced
political obstacles of so overwhelming a character. None evinced a more unselfish patriotism. The overturn of Tilley in New Brunswick,
of which we shall hear presently, was a misfortune quickly repaired. The junction of
Brown, Cartier, and Macdonald in Canada
ensured for them comparatively plain sailing.
But the Nova Scotian leader was pitted against
a redoubtable foe in Joseph Howe; for five
years he faced an angry and rebellious province; he gallantly gave up his place in the
first Dominion ministry in order that another
might have it; and at every turn he displayed
those qualities of pluck, endurance, and dex-
terity which compel admiration. The Tuppers
were of Puritan stock.[1] The future prime
minister, a practising physician, had scored
his first political victory at the age of thirty-
four by defeating Howe in Cumberland county.
Throughout his long and notable career, a
superabundance of energy, and a characteristic which may be defined in a favourable
sense as audacity, never failed him.

[1] See *Recollections of Sixty Years in Canada*, p. 2. The
original Tupper in America came out from England in 1635.
Sir Charles Tupper's great-grandfather migrated from Con-
necticut to Nova Scotia in 1763.

When the motion was presented to appoint
delegates to a conference at Charlottetown, to
consider a legislative union for the three maritime provinces, the skies were serene. The
idea met with a general, if rather languid,
approval. There was not even a flavour of
partisanship about the proceedings, and the
delegates were impartially selected from both
sides. The great Howe regarded the project
with a benignant eye. At this time he was
the Imperial fishery commissioner, and it
was his duty to inspect the deep-sea fishing
grounds each summer in a vessel of the
Imperial Navy. He was invited to go to
Charlottetown as a delegate, and declined in
the following terms :

I am sorry for many reasons to be compelled to decline participation in the conference at Charlottetown. The season is
so far advanced that I find my summer's
work would be so seriously deranged by
the visit to Prince Edward Island that,
without permission from the Foreign Office,
I would scarcely be justified in consulting
my own feelings at the expense of the
public service. I shall be home in October,
and will be very happy to co-operate in

carrying out any measure upon which the conference shall agree.

A more striking evidence of his mood at this juncture is afforded by a speech which he delivered at Halifax in August, when a party of visitors from Canada were being entertained at dinner.

I am not one of those who thank God that I am a Nova Scotian merely, for I am a Canadian as well. I have never thought I was a Nova Scotian, but I have looked across the broad continent as the great territory which the Almighty has given us for an inheritance, and studied the mode by which it could be consolidated, the mode by which it could be united, the mode by which it could be made strong and vigorous while the old flag still floats over the soil.[1]

In the time close at hand Howe was to find these words quoted against him. Meanwhile they were a sure warrant for peace and harmony.

In addressing the Assembly Tupper stated that his visit to Canada during the previous

[1] *The Speeches and Public Letters of Joseph Howe,* edited by J. A. Chisholm, vol. ii, p. 433. Halifax, 1909.

year had convinced him that for some time
the larger union was impracticable. He had
found in Upper Canada a disinclination to
unite with the Maritime Provinces because,
from their identity of interest and geographical
position, they would strengthen Lower Canada.
Lower Canada was equally averse from union
through fear that it would increase the English
influence in a common legislature. Tupper
favoured the larger scheme, and looked forward to its future realization, which would be
helped, not hindered, by the union of the
Maritime Provinces as a first step. Other
speakers openly declared for a general union,
and consented to the Charlottetown gathering
as a convenient preliminary. The resolution
passed without a division; and, though the
members expressed a variety of opinion on
details, there was no hint of a coming storm.

The conference opened at Charlottetown on
September 1, the following delegates being
present: from Nova Scotia, Charles Tupper,
William A. Henry, Robert B. Dickey, Jonathan
McCully, Adams G. Archibald; from New
Brunswick, S. L. Tilley, John M. Johnston,
John Hamilton Gray, Edward B. Chandler,
W. H. Steeves; from Prince Edward Island,
J. H. Gray, Edward Palmer, W. H. Pope,

George Coles, A. A. Macdonald. Newfoundland, having no part in the movement, sent no representatives. Meanwhile Lord Monck, at the request of his ministers, had communicated with the lieutenant-governors asking that a delegation of the Canadian Cabinet might attend the meeting and lay their own plans before it. This was readily accorded. The visitors from Canada arrived from Quebec by steamer. They were George Brown, John A. Macdonald, Alexander T. Galt, George E. Cartier, Hector L. Langevin, William McDougall, D'Arcy McGee, and Alexander Campbell. No official report of the proceedings ever appeared. It is improbable that any exists, but we know from many subsequent references nearly everything of importance that took place. On the arrival of the Canadians they were invited to address the convention at once. The delegates from the Maritime Provinces took the ground that their own plan might, if adopted, be a bar to the larger proposal, and accordingly suggested that the visitors should be heard first. The Canadians, however, saw no reason to fear the smaller union. They believed that Confederation would gain if the three provinces by the sea could be treated as a single unit.

But, being requested to state their case, they naturally had no hesitation in doing so. During the previous two months the members of the coalition must have applied themselves diligently to all the chief points in the project. It may be supposed that Galt, Brown, and Macdonald made a strong impression at Charlottetown. They spoke respectively on the finance, the general parliament, and the constitutional structure of the proposed federation. These subjects contained the germs of nearly all the difficulties. When the delegates reassembled a month later at Quebec, it is clear, from the allusions made in the scanty reports that have come down to us, that the leading phases of the question had already been frankly debated.

Having heard the proposals of Canada, the delegates of the Maritime Provinces met separately to debate the question that had brought them together. Obstacles at once arose. Only Nova Scotia was found to be in favour of the smaller union. New Brunswick was doubtful, and Prince Edward Island positively refused to give up her own legislature and executive. The federation project involved no such sacrifice; and, as Aaron's rod swallowed up all the others, the dazzling prospects held out by Canada eclipsed the other proposal, since they provided a strong central government without destroying the identity of the component parts. The conference decided to adjourn to Halifax, where, at the public dinner given to the visitors, Macdonald made the formal announcement that the delegates were unanimous in thinking that a federal union could be effected. The members, however, kept the secrets of the convention with some skill. The speeches at Halifax, and later on at St John, whither the party repaired, abounded in glowing passages descriptive of future expansion, but were sparing of intimate detail. A passage in Brown's speech at Halifax created favourable comment on both sides of the ocean.

In these colonies as heretofore governed [he said] we have enjoyed great advantages under the protecting shield of the mother country. We have had no army or navy to sustain, no foreign diplomacy to sustain, —our whole resources have gone to our internal improvement,—and notwithstanding our occasional strifes with the Colonial Office, we have enjoyed a degree of self-government and generous consideration such as no colonies in ancient or modern history ever enjoyed at the hands of a

parent state. Is it any wonder that
thoughtful men should hesitate to countenance a step that might change the happy
and advantageous relations we have occupied towards the mother country? I am
persuaded there never was a moment in the
history of these colonies when the hearts
of our people were so firmly attached to
the parent state by the ties of gratitude
and affection as at this moment, and for
one I hesitate not to say that did this movement for colonial union endanger the connection that has so long and so happily
existed, it would have my firm opposition.

These and other utterances, equally forceful
and appealing directly to the pride and ambition of the country, were not without effect in
moulding public opinion. The tour was a
campaign of education. By avoiding the constitutional issues the delegates gave little information which could afford carping critics
an opportunity to assail the movement pre-
maturely. It is true, some sarcastic comments
were made upon the manner in which the
Canadians had walked into the convention and
taken possession. At the Halifax dinner the
governor of Nova Scotia, Sir Richard Graves

Macdonnell, dropped an ironical remark on the 'disinterested' course of Canada, which plainly betrayed his own attitude. But the gathering was, in the main, highly successful and augured well for the movement.

The Charlottetown Conference was therefore an essential part of the proceedings which culminated at Quebec. The ground had been broken. The leaders in the various provinces had formed ties of intimacy and friendship and favourably impressed each other. At this time were laid the foundations of the alliance between Macdonald and Tilley, the Liberal leader in New Brunswick, which made it possible to construct the first federal ministry on a non-party basis and which enlisted in the national service a devoted and trustworthy public man. Tilley's career had few blemishes from its beginning to its end. He was a direct descendant of John Tilley, one of the English emigrants to Massachusetts in the *Mayflower*, and a great-grandson of Samuel Tilley, one of the Loyalists who removed to New Brunswick after the War of Independence. He had been drawn into politics against his wishes by the esteem and confidence of his fellow-citizens. A nominating convention at which he was not present had selected him for the legislature, and his first election had taken place during his absence from the country. Yet he had risen to be prime minister of his province ; and his was the guiding hand which brought New Brunswick into the union. His defeat at first and the speedy reversal of the verdict against Confederation form one of the most diverting episodes in the history of the movement.

The ominous feature of the Charlottetown Conference was the absence of Joseph Howe, the most popular leader in Nova Scotia. This was one of the accidents which so often disturb the calculations of statesmen. When the delegates resumed their labours at Quebec he was in Newfoundland, and he returned home to find that a plan had been agreed upon without his aid. From him, as well as from the governors of Nova Scotia and New Brunswick, the cause of federation was to receive its next serious check.

CHAPTER VI

THE QUEBEC CONFERENCE

THE Quebec Conference began its sessions on the 10th of October 1864. It was now the task of the delegates to challenge and overcome the separatist tendencies that had dominated British America since the dismemberment of the Empire eighty years before. They were to prove that a new nationality could be created, which should retain intact the connection with the mother country. For an event of such historic importance no better setting could have been chosen than the Ancient Capital, with its striking situation and its hallowed memories of bygone days. The delegates were practical and experienced men of affairs, but they lacked neither poetic and imaginative sense nor knowledge of the past ; and it may well be that their labours were inspired and their deliberations influenced by the historic associations of the place.

The gathering was remarkable for the varied

talents and forceful character of its principal members. And here it may be noted that the constitution was not chiefly the product of legal minds. Brown, Tilley, Galt, Tupper, and others who shared largely in the work of construction were not lawyers. The conference represented fairly the different interests and occupations of a young country. It is to be recorded, too, that the conclusions reached were criticized as the product of men in a hurry. Edward Goff Penny, editor of the Montreal *Herald*, a keen critic, and afterwards a senator, complained that the actual working period of the conference was limited to fourteen days. Joseph Howe poured scorn upon Ottawa as the capital, stating that he preferred London, the seat of empire, where there were preserved ' the archives of a nationality not created in a fortnight.' Still more vigorous were the protests against the secrecy of the discussions. A number of distinguished journalists, including several English correspondents who had come across the ocean to write about the Civil War, were in Quebec, and they were disposed to find fault with the precautions taken to guard against publicity. The following memorial was presented to the delegates :

The undersigned, representatives of English and Canadian newspapers, find that it would be impossible for them satisfactorily to discharge their duties if an injunction of secrecy be imposed on the conference and stringently carried into effect. They, therefore, beg leave to suggest whether, while the remarks of individual members of your body are kept secret, the propositions made and the treatment they meet with, might not advantageously be made public, and whether such a course would not best accord with the real interests committed to the conference. Such a kind of compromise between absolute secrecy and unlimited publicity is usually, we believe, observed in cases where an European congress holds the peace of the world and the fate of nations in its hands. And we have thought that the British American Conference might perhaps consider the precedent not inapplicable to the present case. Such a course would have the further advantage of preventing ill-founded and mischievous rumours regarding the proceedings from obtaining currency.[1]

[1] Pope's *Confederation Documents.*

This ingenious appeal was signed by S. Phillips Day, of the London *Morning Herald*, by Charles Lindsey of the Toronto *Leader*, and by Brown Chamberlain of the Montreal *Gazette*. Among the other writers of distinction in attendance were George Augustus Sala of the London *Daily Telegraph*, Charles Mackay of *The Times*, Livesy of *Punch*, and George Brega of the New York *Herald*. But the conference stood firm, and the impatient correspondents were denied even the mournful satisfaction of brief daily protocols. They were forced to be content with overhearing the burst of cheering from the delegates when Macdonald's motion proposing federation was unanimously adopted. The reasons for maintaining strict secrecy were thus stated by John Hamilton Gray,[1] a delegate from New Brunswick, who afterwards became the historian of the Confederation movement :

After much consideration it was determined, as in Prince Edward Island, that the convention should hold its delibera-

[1] There were two delegates named John Hamilton Gray, one whose views are quoted here, the other the prime minister of Prince Edward Island. Only one volume of Gray's work on Confederation ever appeared, the second volume, it is said, being unfinished when the author died in British Columbia.

tions with closed doors. In addition to
the reasons which had governed the convention at Charlottetown, it was further
urged, that the views of individual members,
after a first expression, might be changed
by the discussion of new points, differing
essentially from the ordinary current of
subjects that came under their consideration in the more limited range of the Provincial Legislatures ; and it was held that
no man ought to be prejudiced, or be liable
to the charge in public that he had on some
other occasion advocated this or that doctrine, or this or that principle, inconsistent
with the one that might then be deemed
best, in view of the future union to be
adopted. . . . Liberals and Conservatives
had there met to determine what was best
for the future guidance of half a continent,
not to fight old party battles, or stand by
old party cries, and candour was sought
for more than mere personal triumph. The
conclusion arrived at, it is thought, was
judicious. It ensured the utmost freedom of debate; the more so, inasmuch as
the result would be in no way binding
upon those whose interests were to be
affected until and unless adopted after the

greatest publicity and the fullest public discussions.

That the conference decided wisely admits of no doubt. The provincial secretaries of the several provinces were appointed joint secretaries, and Hewitt Bernard, chief clerk of the department of the attorney-general for Upper Canada, was named executive secretary. In his longhand notes, found among the papers of Sir John Macdonald, and made public thirty years later by Sir Joseph Pope, we have the only official record of the resolutions and debates of the conference. Posterity has reason to be grateful for even this limited revelation of the proceedings from day to day. It enables us to form an idea of the difficulties overcome and of the currents of opinion which combined to give the measure its final shape. No student of Canadian constitutional history will leave unread a single note thus fortunately preserved. The various draft motions, we are told by Sir Joseph Pope, are nearly all in the handwriting of those who moved them, and it was evidently the intention to prepare a complete record. The conference was, however, much hurried at the close. When it began, Sir Etienne Taché, prime minister of Canada, was unanimously elected chairman.[1] Each province was given one vote, except that Canada, as consisting of two divisions, was allowed two votes. After the vote on any motion was put, the delegates of a province might retire for consultation among themselves.   The conference sat as if in committee of the whole, so as to permit of free discussion and suggestion.   The resolutions, having been passed in committee of the whole, were to be reconsidered and carried as if parliament were sitting with the speaker in the chair.

The first motion, which was offered by Macdonald and seconded by Tilley, read : *That the*

---

[1] A list of the delegates, who are now styled the Fathers of Confederation, follows :

From Canada, twelve delegates—SIR ETIENNE P. TACHÉ, receiver-general and minister of Militia ; JOHN A. MACDONALD, attorney-general for Upper Canada ; GEORGE E. CARTIER, attorney-general for Lower Canada ; GEORGE BROWN, president of the Executive Council ; OLIVER MOWAT, postmaster-general ; ALEXANDER T. GALT, minister of Finance ; WILLIAM McDOUGALL, provincial secretary ; T. D'ARCY McGEE, minister of Agriculture ; ALEXANDER CAMPBELL, commissioner of Crown Lands ; J. C. CHAPAIS, commissioner of Public Works ; HECTOR L. LANGEVIN, solicitor-general for Lower Canada ; JAMES COCKBURN, solicitor-general for Upper Canada.

From Nova Scotia, five delegates—CHARLES TUPPER, provincial secretary ; WILLIAM A. HENRY, attorney-general ; R. B. DICKEY, member of the Legislative Council ; JONATHAN McCULLY, member of the Legislative Council ; ADAMS G. ARCHIBALD, member of the Legislative Assembly.

From New Brunswick, seven delegates—SAMUEL LEONARD

best interests and present and future prosperity of British North America will be promoted by a federal union under the crown of Great Britain, provided such union can be effected on principles just to the several provinces. This motion, general in its terms, asserted the principle which the conference had met to decide. It passed unanimously amid much enthusiasm. To support it, one may think, involved no serious responsibility, since any province could at a later stage raise objections to any methods proposed in carrying out the principle. But to secure the hearty and unanimous acceptance of a federal union, as the basis on which the provinces were ready to coalesce, was really to submit the whole issue to the crucial test.

TILLEY, provincial secretary; WILLIAM H. STEEVES, minister without portfolio; J. M. JOHNSTON, attorney-general; PETER MITCHELL, minister without portfolio; E. B. CHANDLER, member of the Legislative Council; JOHN HAMILTON GRAY, member of the Legislative Assembly; CHARLES FISHER, member of the Legislative Assembly.

From Prince Edward Island, seven delegates—COLONEL JOHN HAMILTON GRAY, president of the Council; EDWARD PALMER, attorney-general; WILLIAM H. POPE, colonial secretary; A. A. MACDONALD, member of the Legislative Council; GEORGE COLES, member of the Legislative Assembly; T. HEATH HAVILAND, member of the Legislative Assembly; EDWARD WHELAN, member of the Legislative Assembly.

From Newfoundland, two delegates—F. B. T. CARTER, speaker of the Legislative Assembly; AMBROSE SHEA.

Macdonald's motion reflects, in its careful and comprehensive phrasing, the skill in parliamentary tactics of which he had, during many years, displayed so complete a mastery. To commit the conference at the outset to endorsement of the general principle was to render subsequent objection on some detail, however important, extremely difficult for earnest and broad-minded patriots. The two small provinces might withdraw from the scheme, as they subsequently did, but the larger provinces, led by men of the calibre of Tupper and Tilley, would feel that any subsequent obstacle must be of gigantic proportions if it could not be overcome by statesmanship. After cheerfully taking this momentous step, which irresistibly drove them on to the next, the conference proceeded to discuss Brown's motion proposing the form the federation was to assume. There was to be a general government dealing with matters common to all, and in each province a local government having control of local matters. The second motion was likewise unanimously concurred in. Having, as it were, planted two feet firmly on the ground, the conference was now in a good position to stand firmly against divergences of view, provincial rivalries, and extreme demands.

CHAPTER VII

THE RESULTS OF THE CONFERENCE

THE constitution which the founders of the Dominion devised was the first of its kind on a great scale within the Empire. No English precedents therefore existed. Yet their chief aim was to preserve the connection with Great Britain, and to perpetuate in North America the institutions and principles which the mother of parliaments, during her splendid history, had bequeathed to the world. The Fathers could look to Switzerland, to New Zealand, to the American Republic, and to those experiments and proposals in ancient or modern times which seemed to present features to imitate or examples to avoid.[1] But they were guided, perforce, by the special conditions with which they had to deal. If they had been free to make a perfect contribution to the science of government, the constitution might have been

---

[1] D'Arcy McGee published a treatise in 1865 entitled *Notes on Federal Government Past and Present,* presenting a useful summary of the various constitutions.

different.   It is, of course, true of all existing
federations that they were determined largely
by the relations and circumstances of the combining states.   This is illustrated by compar-
ing the Canadian constitution with those of
the two most notable unions which followed.
Unlike Canada, Australia preferred to leave
the residue of powers to the individual states,
while South Africa adopted a legislative instead of a federal union.   For Canada, a legislative union was impracticable.   This was due
partly to the racial solidarity of the French,
but even more largely to the fully developed
individualism of each province.   It is to the
glory of the Fathers of Confederation that the
constitution, mainly constructed by themselves as the product of their own experience
and reflection, has lasted without substantial
change for nearly half a century.   They were
forced to deal with conditions which they had
not created, yet could not ignore—conditions
which had long perplexed both Imperial and
colonial statesmen, and had rendered government ineffective if not impossible.   They
found the remedy ; and the result is seen in
the powerful and thriving nationality which
their labours evolved.

To set up a strong central government was

the desire of many of the delegates. Macdonald, as has been recorded already, had contended for this in 1861. He argued to the same effect at the conference. The Civil War in the United States, just concluded, had revealed in startling fashion the dangers arising from an exaggerated state sovereignty. 'We must,' he said, 'reverse this process by strengthening the general government and conferring on the provincial bodies only such powers as may be required for local purposes.' When Chandler of New Brunswick perceived with acuteness that in effect this would mean legislative union, Macdonald, as we gather from the fragmentary notes of his speech, made an impassioned appeal for a carefully defined central authority.

I think [he declared] the whole affair would fail and the system be a failure if we adopted Mr Chandler's views. We should concentrate the power in the federal government and not adopt the decentralization of the United States. Mr Chandler would give sovereign power to the local legislatures, just where the United States failed. Canada would be infinitely stronger as she is than under such a system

as proposed by Mr Chandler. It is said
that the tariff is one of the causes of difficulty in the United States. So it would be
with us. Looking at the agricultural interests of Upper Canada, manufacturing of
Lower Canada, and maritime interests of
the lower provinces, in respect to a tariff,
a federal government would be a mediator.
No general feeling of patriotism exists in
the United States. In occasions of difficulty each man sticks to his individual state.
Mr Stephens, the present vice-president
[of the Confederacy], was a strong union
man, yet, when the time came, he went
with his state. Similarly we should stick
to our province and not be British Americans. It would be introducing a source
of radical weakness. It would ruin us in
the eyes of the civilized world. All writers
point out the errors of the United States.
All the feelings prognosticated by Tocque-
ville are shown to be fulfilled.

These and other arguments prevailed.
Several of the most influential delegates were
in theory in favour of legislative union, and
these were anxious to create, as the best
alternative, a general parliament wielding

paramount authority. This object was attained by means of three important clauses in the new constitution : one enumerating the powers of the federal and provincial bodies respectively and assigning the undefined residue to the federal parliament ; another conferring upon the federal ministry the right to dismiss for cause the lieutenant-governors ; and another declaring that any provincial law might, within one year, be disallowed by the central body. Instead of a loosely knit federation, therefore, which might have fallen to pieces at the first serious strain, it was resolved to bring the central legislature into close contact at many points with the individual citizen, and thus raise the new state to the dignity of a nation.

How the designs of the Fathers have been modified by the course of events is well known. The federal power has been restrained from undue encroachment on provincial rights by the decisions, on various issues, of the highest court, the judicial committee of the Imperial Privy Council. The power to dismiss lieutenant-governors was found to be fraught with danger and has been rarely exercised. The dismissal of Letellier, a strong Liberal, from the lieutenant-governorship of Quebec by the

Conservative ministry at Ottawa in 1879, gave rise to some uneasiness and criticism. The reason assigned was that his ' usefulness was gone,' since both houses of parliament had passed resolutions calling for his removal. He was accused of partisanship towards his ministers. The federal prime minister, Sir John Macdonald, assented reluctantly, it is said, to the dismissal. But some of the facts are still obscure. The status of the office and the causes that would warrant removal were thus given by Macdonald at Quebec, according to the imperfect report which has come down to us :

> The office must necessarily be during pleasure. The person may break down, misbehave, etc. . . . The lieutenant-governor will be a very high officer. He should be independent of the federal government, except as to removal for cause, and it is necessary that he should not be removable by any new political party. It would destroy his independence. He should only be removable upon an address from the legislature.

The power of disallowance, the third expedient for curbing the provinces, was exercised with

some freedom down to 1888. In that year a
Quebec measure, the Jesuits' Estates Act,
with a highly controversial preamble calculated to provoke a war of creeds, was not disallowed, although protests were carried past
parliament to the governor-general personally.
The incident directed attention to the previous
practice at Ottawa under both parties and a
new era of non-intervention was inaugurated.
Disallowance is now rare, except where Imperial interests are affected, and never occurs
on the ground of the policy or impolicy of the
measure. The provinces, as a matter of practice, are free within their limits to legislate as
they please. But the Dominion as a self-
governing state has long passed the stage where
the clashing of provincial and federal jurisdictions could shake the constitution.

When the conference, however, considered
provincial powers it went to the root of a
federal system. The maritime delegates as a
whole displayed magnanimity and statesmanship. Brown, as the champion of Upper
Canada, was concerned to see that the interests of his own province were amply secured.
He held radical views. When he spoke, the
calm surface of the conference, where a moderate and essentially conservative constitution-

alism sat entrenched, may have been ruffled.
The following is from the summary which
has been preserved of one of his speeches : [1]

As to local governments, we desire in
Upper Canada that they should not be ex-
pensive, and should not take up political
matters.   We ought not to have two electoral bodies.   Only one body, members to
be elected once in every three years.   Should
have whole legislative power—subject to
lieutenant-governor.   I would have lieutenant-governors appointed by general
government.   It would thus bring these
bodies into harmony with the general
government.   In Upper Canada executive
officers would be attorney-general, trea-
surer, secretary, commissioner of crown
lands and commissioner of public works.
These would form the council of the lieutenant-governor.   I would give lieutenant-
governors veto without advice, but under
certain vote he should be obliged to assent.
During recess lieutenant-governor could
have power to suspend executive officers.
They might be elected for three years or

[1] The quotations in this chapter are taken from Pope's *Confederation Documents*.

otherwise. You might safely allow county councils to appoint other officers than those they do now. One legislative chamber for three years, no power of dissolution, elected on one day in each third year. Departmental officers to be elected during pleasure or for three years. To be allowed to speak but not to vote.

A more suggestive extract than this cannot be found in the discussion. From the astonished Cartier the ejaculation came, ' I entirely differ with Mr Brown. It introduces in our local bodies republican institutions.' From the brevity of the report we cannot gather the whole of Brown's meaning. Apparently his aim was a strictly businesslike administration of provincial affairs, under complete popular control, but with the executive functions as far removed from party domination as erring human nature would permit. There may be seen here points of resemblance to an American state constitution, but Brown was no more a republican than was Napoleon. He was, like Macdonald, an Imperialist who favoured the widest national expansion for Canada. The idea of a republic, either in the abstract or the concrete, had no friends in the

conference. Galt believed independence the
proper aim for a young state, but we find him
stating later : ' We were and are willing to
spend our last men and our last shilling for
our mother country.' [1]   Many years after Confederation Sir Oliver Mowat declared independence the remote goal to keep in view. These
opinions were plainly speculative. Neither
statesman took any step towards carrying
them out, but benevolently left them as a
legacy, unencumbered by conditions, to a
distant posterity.

At the conference Mowat was active to
strengthen the central authority, as also was
Brown. But there was general agreement, despite Brown's plea for a change, that the local
governments should take the form preferred
by themselves and that ministerial responsibility on the British model should prevail
throughout. Upon the question of assigning
the same subjects, such as agriculture, to both
federal and provincial legislatures, Mowat said:

The items of agriculture and immigration
should be vested in both federal and local
governments. Danger often arises where
there is exclusive jurisdiction and not so

[1] At Cornwall, March 2, 1866.

often in cases of concurrent jurisdiction. In
municipal matters the county and township
council often have concurrent jurisdiction.

In the famous contests for provincial rights
which he was afterwards to wage before the
courts, and always successfully, Mowat was
not necessarily forgetful that he himself moved
for the power of disallowance over provincial
laws to be given to the federal authority. With
the caution and clearness of mind that governed
his political course, he naturally made sure of
his ground before fighting, and could thus safely
break a lance with the federal government.
The provincial constitutions were, therefore,
left to be determined by the provinces themselves, and this freedom to modify them con-
tinues, 'except as regards the office of lieutenant-governor.' No province has yet proposed any constitutional change which could
be regarded as an infringement of the inviolacy
of that office, and no circumstances have
arisen to throw light upon the kind of measure
which would be so regarded.[1]

One more point, touching upon provincial
autonomy, deserves to be noticed. In the

[1] It is worth noting that almost any change of importance
would affect the office of the lieutenant-governor and thus
challenge federal interference.

resolutions of the conference, as well as in the British North America Act, the laws passed by the local legislatures are reviewable for one year by the *governor-general*, not by the *governor-general in council*. The colonial secretary drew attention in 1876 to this distinction in the expressions used, and suggested that it was intended to place the responsibility of deciding the validity of provincial laws upon the governor-general personally. The able and convincing memoranda in reply were composed by Edward Blake, the Canadian minister of Justice. He contended that under the letter and spirit of the constitution ministers must be responsible for the governor's action. His view prevailed, and thus within ten years after Confederation the principle that the crown's representative must act only through his advisers on all Canadian matters was maintained. There was nothing in the available records in 1876 to explain why the term 'governor-general' instead of 'governor-general in council' was employed.[1] It is,

[1] We know now from Sir Joseph Pope's *Confederation Documents* (p. 140) that it was proposed in the first draft of the union bill to have interpretation clauses, and one of these declared that where the governor-general was required to do any act it was to be assumed that he performed it by the advice and consent of his executive council.

however, an unassailable principle that the control of the crown over the Canadian provinces can be exercised only through the federal authorities.

When the conference had accepted the outline of the federal and provincial constitutions the danger points might reasonably have been considered past. But there remained to be discussed the representation in the federal parliament and the financial terms. These were the rocks on which the ship nearly split. Representation by population in the proposed House of Commons had been agreed upon at Charlottetown; but when the Prince Edward Island delegates saw that, with sixty-five members for Lower Canada as a fixed number, the proportion assigned to the Island would be five members only, they objected. They were dismayed by the prospect, and when the financial proposals also proved unsatisfactory, their discontent foreshadowed the ultimate withdrawal of the province from the scheme. The other provinces accepted without demur the basis of representation in the new House of Commons.

The composition of the Senate, however, brought on a crisis. 'We were very near broken up,' wrote Brown in a private letter on

October 17, ' on the question of the distribu-
tion of members in the upper chamber of the
federal legislature, but fortunately we have
this morning got the matter amicably com-
promised, after a loss of three days in discussing it.'   The difficulty seems to have been to
select the members of the first Senate with due
regard to party complexion, so as not to
operate in Upper Canada, as Brown felt, unfairly against the Liberals.   Finally, an agreement was arranged on the basis that the
senators should be drawn from both parties ;
and this was ultimately carried out.

A far more important point, whether the
second chamber should be nominated or
elected, caused less debate. Macdonald opened
the discussion with his usual diplomacy :

> With respect to the mode of appoint-
> ments to the Upper House, some of us are
> in favour of the elective principle. More
> are in favour of appointment by the crown.
> I will keep my own mind open on that
> point as if it were a new question to me
> altogether. At present I am in favour of
> appointment by the crown. While I do
> not admit that the elective principle has
> been a failure in Canada, I think we had

better return to the original principle, and in the words of Governor Simcoe endeavour to make ours ' an image and transcript of the British constitution.'

Differing on other issues, Brown and Macdonald were at one on this. They were opposed to a second set of general elections, partly because it would draw too heavily on the organizations and funds of the parties. As an instance of the stability of Brown's views, it should be remembered that he never, at any period, approved of an elective second chamber. The other Liberal ministers from Upper Canada, Mowat and McDougall, stood by the elective system, but the conference voted it down. The Quebec correspondence of the *Globe* at this time throws some light on the reasons for the decision : ' Judging from the tone of conversation few delegates are in favour of election. The expense of contesting a division is enormous and yearly increases. The consequence is there is great difficulty in getting fit candidates, and the tendency is to seek corrupt aid from the administration of the day. There is also fear of a collision between two houses equally representing the people. It is less important to us than to the

French. Why should we not then let Lower Canada, which desires to place a barrier against aggression by the west, decide the question and make her defensive powers as strong as she likes? It would be no great stretch of liberality on our part to accord it to her.' During the debates on Confederation in the Canadian Assembly, in the following year, Macdonald derided the notion that a government would ever ' overrule the independent opinion of the Upper House by filling it with a number of its partisans and political supporters.' This, however, is precisely what has taken place. The Senate is one of the few unsatisfactory creations of the Fathers of Confederation.[1]

The question of the financial terms was surrounded with difficulties. The Maritime Provinces, unlike Upper Canada, were without the municipal organization which provides for local needs by direct taxation. With them

[1] In the copy of the Confederation debates possessed by the writer there appears on the margin of the page, in William McDougall's handwriting and initialled by himself, these words : ' In the Quebec Conference I moved and Mr Mowat seconded a motion for the elective principle. About one-third of the delegates voted for the proposition, Brown arguing and voting against it. At this date (1887) under Sir John's policy and action the Senate contains only 14 Liberals ; all his appointments being made from his own party.'

SIR JOHN A. MACDONALD

From the painting by A. Dickson Patterson

the provincial government was a nursing mother and paid for everything. Out of the general revenue came the money for bridges, roads, schools, wharves, piers, and other improvements, in addition to the cost of maintaining the fiscal, postal, and other charges of the province. The revenue was raised by customs duties, sales of crown lands, royalties, or export duties. The devotion to indirect taxation, which is not absent from provinces with municipal bodies, was to them an all-absorbing passion. The Canadian delegates were unsympathetic. John Hamilton Gray describes the scene :

> Agreement seemed hopeless, and on or about the tenth morning, after the convention met, the conviction was general that it must break up without coming to any conclusion. The terms of mutual concession and demand had been drawn to their extremest tension and silence was all around. At last a proposition was made that the convention should adjourn for the day, and that in the meantime the finance ministers of the several provinces should meet, discuss the matter amongst themselves, and see if they could not agree upon something.[1]

[1] Gray's *Confederation*, p. 62.

On this committee were Brown and Galt acting for Canada, while the others were Tupper, Tilley, Archibald, Pope, and Shea. The scheme set forth in the resolutions was the result. It need not be detailed, but the sixty-fourth resolution, on which was centred the keenest criticism, reads as follows :

> In consideration of the transfer to the general parliament of the powers of taxation, an annual grant in aid of each province shall be made, equal to 80 cents per head of the population as established by the census of 1861, the population of Newfoundland being estimated at 130,000. Such aid shall be in full settlement of all future demands upon the general government for local purposes and shall be paid half-yearly in advance to each province.

The system of provincial subsidies has often been denounced. The delegates may have thought that they had shut the door to further claims, but the finality of the arrangement was soon tested, and in 1869 Nova Scotia received better terms. There were increases in the subsidies to the provinces on several subsequent occasions, and no one believes the end has yet been reached. The growing needs of the provinces and the general aversion from direct taxation furnish strong temptations to make demands upon the federal treasury.

The conference, after adopting the seventy-two resolutions embodying the basis of the union, agreed that the several governments should submit them to the respective legislatures at the ensuing session. They were to be carried *en bloc*, lest any change should entail a fresh conference. The delegates made a tour of Canada, visiting Montreal, Ottawa, and Toronto, where receptions and congratulations awaited them. Their work had been done quickly. It had now to run the gauntlet of parliamentary discussion.

CHAPTER VIII

THE DEBATES OF 1865

In the province of Canada no time was lost in placing the new constitution before parliament. A dilatory course would have been unwise. The omens were favourable. Such opposition as had developed was confined to Lower Canada. The Houses met in January 1865, and the governor-general used this language in his opening speech :

With the public men of British North America it now rests to decide whether the vast tract of country which they inhabit shall be consolidated into a State, combining within its area all the elements of national greatness, providing for the security of its component parts and contributing to the strength and stability of the Empire ; or whether the several Provinces of which it is constituted shall remain in their present fragmentary and isolated condition, comparatively powerless for mutual aid, and incapable of undertaking their proper share of Imperial responsibility.

The procedure adopted was the moving in each House of an address to the Queen praying that a measure might be submitted to the Imperial parliament based upon the Quebec resolutions. The debate began in the Legislative Council on the 3rd of February and in the Assembly three days later. The debate in the popular branch lasted until the 13th of March ; in the smaller chamber it was concluded by the 23rd of February.

These debates, subsequently published in a volume of 1032 pages, are a mirror which reflects for us the political life of the time and the events of the issue under discussion. They set forth the hopes and intentions of the Fathers with reference to their own work ; and if later developments have presented some surprises, some situations which they did not foresee, as was indeed inevitable, their prescience is nowhere shown to have been seriously at fault. Some of the speeches are commonplace ; a few are wearisome ; but many of them are examples of parliamentary eloquence at its best, and the general level is high.

The profound sincerity of the leaders of the

coalition, whether in or out of office, is not to
be questioned. The supporters of the union
bore down all opposition. Macdonald's wonderful tact, Brown's passionate earnestness,
and Galt's mastery of the financial problem,
were never displayed to better advantage ;
while the redoubtable Cartier marshalled his
French compatriots before their timidity had
a chance to assert itself.   Particularly interesting is the attitude which Brown assumed
towards the French.   He had been identified
with a vicious crusade against their race and
creed. Its cruel intolerance cannot be justified,
and every admirer of Brown deplores it.   He
met them now with a frank friendliness which
evoked at once the magnanimity and readi-
ness to forgive that has always marked this
people and is one of their most engaging
qualities.   Said Brown :

The scene presented by this chamber at
this moment, I venture to affirm, has few
parallels in history.   One hundred years
have passed away since these provinces
became by conquest part of the British
Empire.   I speak in no boastful spirit.   I
desire not for a moment to excite a painful
thought.   What was then the fortune of

war of the brave French nation might have
been ours on that well-fought field.   I
recall those olden times merely to mark the
fact that here sit to-day the descendants
of the victors and the vanquished in the
fight of 1759, with all the differences of
language, religion, civil law and social
habit nearly as distinctly marked as they
were a century ago.   Here we sit to-day
seeking amicably to find a remedy for constitutional evils and injustice complained
of.   By the vanquished ?   No, sir, but
complained of by the conquerors ! [French-
Canadian cheers.]

Here sit the representatives of the British
population claiming justice—only justice ;
and here sit the representatives of the
French population, discussing in the French
tongue whether we shall have it.   One hundred years have passed away since the
conquest of Quebec, but here sit the chil-
dren of the victor and the vanquished, all
avowing hearty attachment to the British
Crown, all earnestly deliberating how we
shall best extend the blessings of British
institutions, how a great people may be
established on this continent in close and
hearty connection with Great Britain.

In thus proclaiming the aim and intent of the advocates of Confederation in respect to the Imperial link, Brown expressed the views of all. It was not a cheap appeal for applause, because the question could not be avoided. It came up at every turn. What was the purpose, the critics of the measure asked, of this new constitution ? Did it portend separation ? Would it not inevitably lead to independence ? and if not, why was the term ' a new nationality ' so freely used ? In the opening speech of the debate Macdonald met the issue squarely with the statesmanlike gravity that befitted the occasion :

> No one can look into futurity and say what will be the destiny of this country. Changes come over peoples and nations in the course of ages. But so far as we can legislate, we provide that for all time to come the sovereign of Great Britain shall be the sovereign of British North America.

And he went on to predict that the measure would not tend towards independence, but that the country, as it grew in wealth and population, would grow also in attachment to the crown and seek to preserve it. This prophecy, as we know, has proved true.

The fear of annexation to the United States figured likewise in the debate, but the condition of the Republic, so recently in the throes of civil war, was not such as to give rise to serious apprehension on that score. The national sentiment, however, which would naturally arise when the new state was constituted, was a proper subject for consideration, since it might easily result in a complete, if peaceful, revolution.

There were other uncertain factors in the situation which gave the opponents of Confederation an opportunity for destructive criticism. The measure was subjected to the closest scrutiny by critics who were well qualified to rouse any hostile feeling in the country if such existed. Weighty attacks came from dissentient Liberals like Dorion, Holton, and Sandfield Macdonald. A formidable opponent, too, was Christopher Dunkin, an independent Conservative, inspired, it may be supposed, by the distrust of constitutional change entertained by his immediate fellow-countrymen, the English minority in Lower Canada.

Brown bore the brunt of the attack from erstwhile allies and faced it in this fashion :

No constitution ever framed was without defect ; no act of human wisdom was ever free from imperfection. . . . To assert then that our scheme is without fault, would be folly. It was necessarily the work of concession ; not one of the thirty-three framers but had on some points to yield his opinions ; and, for myself, I freely admit that I struggled earnestly, for days together, to have portions of the scheme amended.

This was reasonable ground to take and drew some of the sting from the criticism.

But all the criticism was not futile. Some of the defects pointed out bore fruit in the years that followed. As already stated, the financial terms were far from final, and a demand for larger subsidies had soon to be met. Friction between the federal and provincial powers arose in due course, but not precisely for the reasons given. The administration of the national business has cost more than was expected, and has not been free, to employ the ugly words used in these debates, from jobbery and corruption. The cost of a progressive railway policy has proved infinitely greater than the highest estimates put forth by the Fathers. The duty of forming a ministry so as to give adequate representation

to all the provinces has been quite as difficult
as Dunkin said it would be.   To parcel out the
ministerial offices on this basis is one of the
unwritten conventions of the constitution, and
has taxed the resources of successive prime
ministers to the utmost.   With all his skill, as
we shall see later, Sir John Macdonald nearly
gave up in despair his first attempt to form a
ministry after Confederation.   Yet it must
be said, surveying the whole field, that the
critics of the resolutions failed to make out a
case.

Both in the Legislative Council and in the
Assembly the resolution for a nominated second
chamber caused much debate.   But the elective principle was not defended with marked
enthusiasm.   By the Act of 1840 which united
the Canadas the Council had been a nominated
body solely.   Its members received no in-
demnity ;   and, as some of them were averse
from the political strife which raged with
special fury until 1850, a quorum could not
always be obtained.   Sir Etienne Taché drew
an affecting picture of the speaker frequently
taking the chair at the appointed time, waiting in stiff and solemn silence for one hour by
the clock, and at last retiring discomfited, since
members enough did not appear to form a

quorum. To remedy the situation the Imperial parliament had passed an Act providing for the election of a portion of the members. Fresh difficulties had then arisen. The electoral divisions had been largely formed by grouping portions of counties together ; the candidates had found that physical endurance and a long purse were as needful to gain a seat in the Council as a patriotic interest in public affairs ; and it had become difficult to secure candidates. This unsatisfactory experience of an elective upper chamber made it comparatively easy to carry the resolution providing for a nominated Senate in the new constitution.

The agreement that the resolutions must be accepted or rejected as a whole led Dorion to complain that the power of parliament to amend legislation was curtailed. What value had the debate, if the resolutions were in the nature of a treaty and could not be moulded to suit the wishes of the people's representatives ? The grievance was not so substantial as it appeared. The Imperial parliament, which was finally to pass the measure, could be prompted later on to make any alterations strongly desired by Canadian public opinion.

Why were not the terms of Confederation

submitted to the Canadian people for ratification? The most strenuous fight was made in parliament on this point, and in after years, too, constitutional writers, gifted with the wisdom which comes after the event, have declared the omission a serious error. Goldwin Smith observed that Canadians might conceivably in the future discard their institutions as lacking popular sanction when they were adopted, seeing that in reality they were imposed on the country by a group of politicians and a distant parliament. In dealing with such objections the reasons given at the time must be considered. The question was discussed at the Quebec Conference, doubtless informally.[1] The constitutional right of the legislatures to deal with the matter was unquestioned by the Canadian members. Shortly after the conference adjourned, Galt in a speech at Sherbrooke [2] declared that, if during the discussion of the scheme in parliament any serious doubt arose respecting the public feeling on the subject, the people would be called upon to decide for themselves. The

[1] See the remark of McCully of Nova Scotia that the delegates should take the matter into their own hands and not wait to educate the people up to it.—Pope's *Confederation Documents*, p. 60.

[2] November 23, 1864.

Globe, which voiced the opinion of Brown, said :

> If on the assembling of Parliament the majority in that body in favour of Confederation shall be found so large as to make it manifest that any reference to the country would simply be a matter of form, Ministers will not, we take it, feel warranted in putting the country to great trouble and expense for the sake of that unessential formality.

When challenged in parliament the government gave its reasons. The question of Confederation had, in one form or another, been before the country for years. During 1864 there had been elections in eleven ridings for the Assembly and in fourteen for the Legislative Council. The area of country embraced by these contests included forty counties. Of the candidates in these elections but four opposed federation and only two of them were elected. Brown stated impetuously that not five members of parliament in Upper Canada dare go before the people against the scheme. No petitions against it were presented, and its opponents had not ventured to hold meetings, knowing that an enormous majority of the

people favoured it.   This evidence, in Upper
Canada, was accepted as conclusive.   In Lower
Canada appearances were not quite so convincing.   The ministry representing that section was not a coalition, and the Liberal leaders,
both French and English, organized an agitation.   But afterwards, in the campaign of
1867, Cartier swept all before him.   It was
also argued that parliament was fresh from
the people as recently as 1864, and that though
the mandate to legislate was not specific, it
was sufficient.   The method of ascertaining the
popular verdict by means of a referendum was
proposed, but rejected as unknown to the constitution and at variance with British practice.

Parliament finally adopted the resolutions
by a vote of ninety-one to thirty-three in the
Assembly and of forty-five to fifteen in the
Legislative Council.   Hillyard Cameron, politically a lineal descendant of the old Family
Compact, supported by Matthew Crooks
Cameron, a Conservative of the highest integrity and afterwards chief justice, then moved
for a reference to the people by a dissolution
of parliament.   But after an animated debate
the motion was defeated, and no further efforts
in this direction were attempted.   That an
eagerness to invoke the judgment of democracy

was not seen at its best, when displayed by two Tories of the old school, may justify the belief that parliamentary tactics, rather than the pressure of public opinion, inspired the move.

Fortune had smiled upon the statesmen of the Canadian coalition. In a few months they had accomplished wonders. They had secured the aid of the Maritime Provinces in drafting a scheme of union. They had made tours in the east and the west to prepare public opinion for the great stroke of state. They and their co-delegates had formulated and adopted the Quebec resolutions, on which a chorus of congratulation had drowned, for the time, the voices of warning and expostulation. And, finally, the ministers had met parliament and had secured the adoption of their scheme by overwhelming majorities.

But all was not so fair in the provinces by the sea. Before the Canadian legislature prorogued, the Tilley government had been hurled from power in New Brunswick, Joseph Howe was heading a formidable agitation in Nova Scotia, and in the other two provinces the cause was lost. It seemed as if a storm had burst that would overwhelm the union and that the hands of the clock would be put back.

CHAPTER IX

ROCKS IN THE CHANNEL

In the month of March 1865, as the Canadian debates drew to a close, ominous reports began to arrive from all the Maritime Provinces. An election campaign of unusual bitterness was going on in New Brunswick. The term of the legislature would expire in the following June ; and the Tilley government had decided to dissolve and present the Quebec resolutions to a newly elected legislature, a blunder in tactics due, it may be, to over-confidence. The secrecy which had shrouded the proceedings of the delegates at first was turned to account by their opponents, who set in motion a campaign of mendacity and misrepresentation. The actual terms became known too late to counteract this hostile agitation, which had been systematically carried on throughout the province. The bogey employed to stampede the electors was direct taxation. The farmers were told that every cow or horse they possessed, even the chickens in the farmyard, would be taxed for the benefit of Canada. Worse than all, it was contended, the bargain struck at the honour of the province, because, as the subsidy was on the basis of paying to the provinces annually eighty cents per head of population, the people were really being sold by the government like sheep for this paltry price. The trusted Tilley, easily first in popular affection by reason of his probity and devotion to public duty, was discredited. His opponent in the city of St John, A. R. Wetmore, illustrated the dire effects of Confederation in an imaginary dialogue, between himself and his young son, after this fashion : ' Father, what country do we live in ? '—and, of course, the reply came promptly—' My dear son, you have no country, for Mr Tilley has sold us all to the Canadians for eighty cents a head.' Time and full discussion would have dissipated the forces of the anti-confederates. But constituencies worked upon by specious appeals to prejudice are notoriously hard to woo during an election struggle. There existed also honest doubts in many minds regarding federation. Enough men of character and influence in both parties joined to form a strong opposition, while one of Tilley's

colleagues in the ministry, George Hathaway,
went over to the enemy at a critical hour.
The agitation swept the province. It was
not firmly rooted in the convictions of the
people, but it sufficed to overwhelm the government. All the Cabinet ministers, including
Tilley, were beaten. And so it happened
that, when the Canadian ministers were in
the full tide of parliamentary success at
home, the startling news arrived that New
Brunswick had rejected federation, and that
in a House of forty-one members only six
supporters of the scheme had been returned
from the polls.

Equally alarming was the prospect in Nova
Scotia. On arriving home from Quebec, Dr
Tupper and his fellow-delegates found a situation which required careful handling. 'When
the delegates returned to the Province,' says
a pamphlet of the time, 'they did not meet
with a very flattering reception. They had no
ovation; and no illuminations, bonfires, and
other demonstrations of felicitous welcome
hailed their return. They were not escorted
to their homes with torches and banners, and
through triumphal arches; no cannon thun-
dered forth a noisy welcome. They were received in solemn, sullen and ominous silence.

No happy smiles greeted them; but they entered the Province as into the house of mourning.' [1] And in Nova Scotia the hostility was not, as in New Brunswick, merely a passing wave of surprise and discontent. It lasted for years. Nor was it, as many think, the sole creation of the ambitious Joseph Howe. It doubtless owed much to his power as a leader of men and his influence over the masses of the Nova Scotians. But there is testimony that this proud and spirited people, with traditions which their origin and history fully warranted them in cherishing, regarded with aversion the prospect of a constitutional revolution, especially one which menaced their political identity. Robert Haliburton has related the results of his observations before the issue had been fairly disclosed and before Howe had emerged from seclusion to take a hand in the game.

In September and October, 1864, when our delegates were at Quebec, and therefore before there could be any objections raised to the details of the scheme, or to the mode of its adoption, I travelled through six

[1] *Confederation Examined in the Light of Reason and Common Sense,* by Martin I. Wilkins.

counties, embracing the whole of Cape
Breton and two counties in Nova Scotia,
and took some trouble to ascertain the
state of public opinion as to what was
taking place, and was greatly surprised at
finding that every one I met, without a
solitary exception, from the highest to the
lowest, was alarmed at the idea of a union
with Canada, and that the combination of
political leaders, so far from recommending
the scheme, filled their partisans with as
much dismay as if the powers of light and
darkness were plotting against the public
safety. It was evident that unless the
greatest tact were exercised, a storm of
ignorant prejudice and alarm would be
aroused, that would sweep the friends of
union out of power, if not out of public life.
The profound secrecy preserved by the delegates as to the scheme, until an accomplice
turned Queen's evidence, added fuel to the
flame, and convinced the most sceptical
that there was a second Gunpowder Plot
in existence, which was destined to annihi-
late our local legislature and our provincial
rights.[1]

[1] *Intercolonial Trade our only Safeguard against Disunion,* by
R. G. Haliburton. Ottawa, 1868.

This was the situation which confronted Howe when he returned in the autumn from his tour as fishery commissioner. He had written from Newfoundland, on hearing of the conference at Charlottetown : ' I have read the proceedings of the delegates and I am glad to be out of the mess.' At first he listened in silence to the Halifax discussions on both sides of the question. These were non-partisan, since Archibald and McCully, the Liberal leaders, were as much concerned in the result as the Conservative ministers. Howe finally broke silence with the first of his articles in the Halifax *Chronicle* on ' The Botheration Scheme.' This gave the signal for an agitation which finally bore Nova Scotia to the verge of rebellion. Howe's course has been censured as the greatest blot upon an otherwise brilliant career. In justice to his memory the whole situation should be examined. He did not start the agitation. Many able and patriotic Nova Scotians urged him on. Favourable to union as an abstract theory he had been : to Confederation as a policy he had never distinctly pledged himself. The idea that the Quebec terms were sacrosanct, and that hostility to them involved disloyalty to the Empire, must be put aside. It is neither necessary nor fair to assume that Howe's conduct was wholly inspired by the spleen and jealousy commonly ascribed to him ; for, with many others, he honestly held the view that the interests of his native province were about to be sacrificed in a bad bargain. Nevertheless, his was a grave political error—an error for which he paid bitterly—which in the end cost him popularity, private friendship, and political reputation. But the noble courage and patience with which he sought to repair it should redeem his fame.[1]

It was no secret that the governor of Nova Scotia, Sir Richard Graves Macdonnell, was opposed to Confederation. The veiled hostility of his speech in Halifax has already been noted ; and he followed it with another at Montreal, after the conference, which revealed a captious mind on the subject. Arthur Hamilton Gordon (afterwards Lord Stanmore), the lieutenant-governor of New Brunswick, also hampered the movement ; although the Imperial instructions, even at this early stage of the proceedings, pointed to an opposite

[1] Howe's biographers have dealt with this episode in his life in a vein of intelligent generosity. See *Joseph Howe* by Mr Justice Longley in the 'Makers of Canada' series and *The Tribune of Nova Scotia,* by Prof. W. L. Grant, in the present Series.

course. In the gossipy diary of Miss Frances Monck, a member of Lord Monck's household at Quebec in 1864, appears this item : ' Sir R. M. is so against this confederation scheme because he would be turned away. He said to John A.: You shall not make a mayor of *me*, I can tell you ! meaning a deputy governor of a province.' Macdonnell was transferred to Hong-Kong; and Gordon, after a visit to England, experienced a change of heart. But the mischief done was incalculable.

In view of the disturbed state of public opinion in Nova Scotia the Tupper government resolved to play a waiting game. When the legislature met in February 1865, the federation issue came before it merely as an open question. The defeat of Tilley in New Brunswick followed soon after, and the occasion was seen to be inopportune for a vote upon union. But, as some action had to be taken, a motion was adopted affirming the previous attitude of the legislature respecting a maritime union. There was a long debate ; Tupper expounded and defended the Quebec resolutions ; but no one seemed disposed to come to close quarters with the question. Tupper's policy was to mark time.

Prince Edward Island made another contribution to the chapter of misfortune by definitely rejecting the proposed union. The Legislative Council unanimously passed a resolution against it, and in the Assembly the adverse vote was twenty-three against five. It was declared that the scheme ' would prove politically, commercially and financially disastrous ' ; and an address to the Queen prayed that no Imperial action should be taken to unite the Island to Canada or any other province.

Newfoundland, likewise, turned a deaf ear to the proposals. The commercial interests of that colony assumed the critical attitude of the same element in Nova Scotia, and objected to the higher customs duties which a uniform tariff for the federated provinces would probably entail. It was resolved to take no action until after a general election ; and the representations made to the legislature by Governor Musgrave produced no effect. Although the governor was sanguine, it required no great power of observation to perceive that the ancient colony would not accept federation.

The Canadian government took prompt measures. On the arrival of the bad news from New Brunswick it was decided to hurry the debates to a close, prorogue parliament, and send a committee of the Cabinet to England to confer with the Imperial authorities on federation, defence, reciprocity, and the acquisition of the North-West Territories. This programme was adhered to. The four ministers who left for England in April were Macdonald, Brown, Galt, and Cartier. The mission, among other results pertinent to the cause of union, secured assurances from the home authorities that every legitimate means for obtaining the early assent of the Maritime Provinces would be adopted.[1] But the calamities of 1865 were not over. The prime minister, Sir Etienne Taché, died ; and Brown refused to serve under either Macdonald or Cartier. He took the ground that the coalition of parties had been held together by a chief (Taché) who had ceased to be actuated by strong party feelings or personal ambitions and in whom all sections reposed confidence. Standing alone, this reasoning is sound in practical politics. Behind it, of course, was the unwillingness of Brown to accept the leadership of his great rival. Macdonald then proposed Sir Narcisse Belleau, one of their colleagues, as leader of the government. Brown assented ; and the coalition was

[1] Report of the Canadian ministers to Lord Monck, July 12, 1865.

reconstituted on the former basis, but not with the old cordiality. The rift within the lute steadily widened, and before the year closed Brown resigned from the ministry. His difference with his colleagues arose, he stated, from their willingness to renew reciprocal trade relations with the United States by concurrent legislation instead of, as heretofore, by a definite treaty. Although his two Liberal associates remained in the ministry, and the vacancy was given to another Liberal, Fergusson Blair, the recrudescence of partisan friction occasioned by the episode was not a good omen. Brown, however, promised continued support of the federation policy until the new constitution should come into effect—a promise which he fulfilled as far as party exigencies permitted. But the outlook was gloomy. There were rocks ahead which might easily wreck the ship. Who could read the future so surely as to know what would happen ?

CHAPTER X

'THE BATTLE OF UNION'

AT the dawn of 1866 the desperate plight of the cause of union called for skilful generalship in four different arenas of political action. In any one of them a false move would have been fatal to success; and there was always the danger that, on so extended a front, the advocates of union might be fighting at cross purposes and so inflicting injury on each other instead of upon the enemy. It was necessary that the Imperial influence should be exerted as far as the issues at stake warranted its employment. Canada, the object of suspicion, must march warily to avoid rousing the hostile elements elsewhere. The unionists of New Brunswick should be given time to recover their position, while those of Nova Scotia should stand ready for instant co-operation.

The judicious but firm attitude of the Imperial authorities was a material factor in the

situation. From 1862 onwards there was no
mistaking the policy of Downing Street, as expressed by the Duke of Newcastle in that year
to the governor of Nova Scotia. Colonial
secretaries came and went and the complexion
of British ministries changed, but the principle of union stood approved. Any proposals,
however, must emanate from the colonies
themselves ; and, when an agreement in whole
or in part should be reached, the proper procedure was indicated. 'The most satisfactory mode,' said the dispatch of 1862, ' of test-
ing the opinion of the people of British North
America would probably be by means of resolution or address proposed in legislatures of
each province by its own government.' This
course all the governments had kept in mind,
with the additional safeguard that the ministers of the day had associated with themselves
the leaders of the parliamentary oppositions.
Nothing could have savoured less of partisanship than the Quebec Conference ; and Mr
Cardwell, the colonial secretary, had acknow-
ledged the resolutions of that body in handsome terms.

The home authorities faced the difficulties
with a statesmanlike front. They had no dis-
position to dictate, but, once assured that a

substantial majority in each consenting province supported the scheme, it was their duty to speak plainly, no matter how vehemently a section of opinion in England or in the provinces protested. They held the opinion, that since the provinces desired to remain within the Empire, they must combine. All the grounds for this belief could not be publicly stated. It was one of those exceptional occasions when Downing Street, by reason of its superior insight into foreign affairs and by full comprehension of the danger then threatening, knew better than the man on the spot. The colonial opposition might be sincere and patriotic, but it was wrong. Heed could not be paid to the agitations in Nova Scotia and New Brunswick because they were founded upon narrow conceptions of statesmanship and erroneous information.

Another difficulty with which British governments, whether Liberal or Tory, had to contend was the separatist doctrine known as that of the Manchester School. When George Brown visited England in 1864 he was startled into communicating with John A. Macdonald in these terms :

I am much concerned to observe—and I

write it to you as a thing that must seriously be considered by all men taking a lead hereafter in Canadian public matters —that there is a manifest desire in almost every quarter that, ere long, the British American colonies should shift for themselves, and in some quarters evident regret that we did not declare at once for independence. I am very sorry to observe this ; but it arises, I hope, from the fear of invasion of Canada by the United States, and will soon pass away with the cause that excites it.

The feeling did pass away in time. The responsible statesmen of that period were forced to go steadily forward and ignore it, just as they refused to be dominated by appeals from colonial reactionaries who abhorred change and who honestly believed that in so doing they exhibited the best form of attachment to the Empire.

Why Mr Arthur Gordon, the lieutenant-governor of New Brunswick, was at first opposed to Confederation, when his ministers were in favour of it, is not quite clear.[1]

[1] Gordon's dispatches to the colonial secretary indicate that from the first he distrusted the Quebec scheme and that the over-

However this may be, his punishment was not long in coming ; and, if he escaped from the storm without loss of honour, he certainly suffered in dignity and comfort. The new ministry which took office in New Brunswick was formed by A. J. Smith, who afterwards as Sir Albert Smith had a useful career in the Dominion parliament. His colleagues had taken a prominent part in the agitation against Confederation, but it appears that they had no very settled convictions on this question, and that they differed on many others. At any rate, dissension soon broke out among them. The colonial secretary pressed upon the province the desirability of the union in terms described as ' earnest and friendly suggestions,' and which left no doubt as to the wishes of the home government. ' You will express,' said the colonial secretary to the lieutenant-governor, ' the strong and deliberate opinion of Her Majesty's Government that it is an object much to be desired that all the British North American colonies should agree to unite in one government.' In stating

throw of his ministers owing to it occasioned him no great grief. James Hannay, the historian, attributes his conduct to chagrin at the pushing aside of maritime union, as he had hoped to be the first governor of the smaller union.

the reasons for this opinion the dispatch continued :

> Looking to the determination which this country has ever exhibited to regard the defence of the colonies as a matter of Imperial concern, the colonies must recognize a right, and even acknowledge an obligation, incumbent on the home government to urge with earnestness and just authority the measures which they consider to be most expedient on the part of the colonies with a view to their own defence.

The New Brunswick frontier, as well as Canada, was disturbed by the threatened Fenian invasion, so that the question of defence was apposite and of vital importance.

Presently a change of sentiment began to show itself in the province, and the shaky Cabinet began to totter from resignations and disagreements. By-elections followed and supporters of federation were returned. The legislature met early in March. In the lieutenant-governor's speech from the throne, a reference to the colonial secretary's dispatch implied that Gordon had changed his views and was now favourable to union. He after-

wards explained that the first minister and
several of his colleagues had privately intimated to him their concurrence, but felt unable
at the time to explain their altered attitude
to the legislature. The next step involved
proceedings still more unusual, if not actually
unconstitutional: the address of the Legislative Council in reply to the speech from the
throne contained a vigorous endorsement of
union; and the lieutenant-governor accepted
it, without consulting his advisers, and in language which left them no recourse but to
resign. A new ministry was formed on the
18th of April, and the House was dissolved.
The ensuing elections resulted in a complete
victory for federation. On the 21st of June
the legislature met, fresh from the people, and
adopted, by a vote of thirty to eight, a resolution appointing delegates to arrange with the
Imperial authorities a scheme of union that
would secure ' the just rights and interests of
New Brunswick.' The battle was won.

Meanwhile, like the mariner who keeps a
vigilant eye upon the weather, the Tupper
government in Nova Scotia observed the proceedings in New Brunswick with a view to
action at the proper moment. The agitation
throughout the province had not affected the

position of parties in the legislature which met in February. The government continued to treat federation as a non-contentious subject. No reference to it was made in the governor's speech, and the legislature occupied itself with other business. The agitation in the country, with Howe leading it, and William Annand, member for East Halifax and editor of the *Chronicle*, as his chief associate, went on. Then the *débâcle* of the anti-confederate party in New Brunswick began to attract attention and give rise to speculations on what would be the action of the Tupper government. This was soon to be disclosed. In April, a few days before the fall of the Smith ministry in New Brunswick, William Miller, member for Richmond, made a speech in the House which was destined to produce a momentous effect. His proposal was to appoint delegates to frame a scheme in consultation with the Imperial authorities, and thus ignore the Quebec resolutions. To these resolutions Miller had been strongly opposed. He had borne a leading part with Howe and Annand in the agitation, although he was always favourable to union in the abstract and careful on all occasions to say so. Now, however, his speech provided a means of enabling Nova Scotia to enter the union with the consent of the legislature, and Tupper was quick to seize the opportunity by putting it in the form of a motion before the House. An extremely bitter debate followed; vigorous epithets were exchanged with much freedom, and Tupper's condemnation of Joseph Howe omitted nothing essential to the record. But at length, at midnight of the 10th of April, the legislature, by a vote of thirty-one to nineteen, adopted the motion which cleared the way for bringing Nova Scotia into the Dominion.

Miller's late allies never forgave his action on this occasion. He was accused of having been bribed to desert them. When he was appointed to the Senate in 1867 the charge was repeated, and many years afterwards was revived in an offensive form. Finally, Miller entered suit for libel against the Halifax *Chronicle*, and in the witness-box Sir Charles Tupper bore testimony to the propriety of Miller's conduct in 1866. Notwithstanding the hostility between Howe and Tupper, they afterwards resumed friendly relations and sat comfortably together in the Dominion Cabinet. In politics hard words can be soon forgotten. The doughty Tupper had won his province for the union and could afford to forget.

SIR CHARLES TUPPER, Bart.
From a photograph by Elliott and Fry, London

The tactics pursued in Canada during these exciting months in the Maritime Provinces were those defined by a great historian, in dealing with a different convulsion, as 'masterly inactivity.' In that memorable speech of years afterwards when Macdonald, about to be overwhelmed by the Pacific Railway charges, appealed to his countrymen in words that came straight from the heart, he declared: 'I have fought the battle of union.' The events of 1866 are the key to this utterance. Parliament was not summoned until June; and meanwhile ministers said nothing. That this line of policy was deliberate, is set forth in a private letter from Macdonald to Tilley:

Had we met early in the year and before your elections, the greatest embarrassment and your probable defeat at the polls would have ensued. We should have been pressed by the Opposition to declare whether we adhered to the Quebec resolutions or not. Had we answered in the affirmative, you would have been defeated, as you were never in a position to go to the polls on those resolutions. Had we replied in the negative, and stated that it was an open question and that the resolutions were liable to alteration, Lower Canada would have arisen as one man, and good-bye to federation.

Thus was the situation saved ; and, although the delegates from the Maritime Provinces were obliged to wait in London for some months for their Canadian colleagues, owing to the Fenian invasion of Canada and to a change of ministry in England, the body of delegates assembled in December at the Westminster Palace Hotel, in London, and sat down to frame the details of the bill for the union of British North America.

CHAPTER XI

THE FRAMING OF THE BILL

WHEN the British American delegates met in London to frame the bill they found themselves in an atmosphere tending to chill their enthusiasm. Lord Palmerston had died the year before, and with him had disappeared an adventurous foreign policy and the militant view of empire. The strictly utilitarian school of thought was dominant. Canada was unpleasantly associated in the minds of British statesmen with the hostile attitude of the United States which seemed to threaten a most unwelcome war. John Bright approved of ceding Canada to the Republic as the price of peace. Gladstone also wrote to Goldwin Smith suggesting this course. The delegates were confronted by the same ideas which had distressed George Brown two years earlier. The colonies were not to be forcibly cast off, but even in official circles the opinion prevailed that ultimate separation was the inevitable end. The reply

of Sir Edward Thornton, the British minister
at Washington, to a proposal that Canada
should be ceded to the United States was merely
that Great Britain could not thus dispose of a
colony ' against the wishes of the inhabitants.'
These lukewarm views made no appeal to the
delegates and the young communities they
represented. It was their aim to propound a
method of continuing the connection. Theirs
was not the vision of a military sway intended
to overawe other nations and to revive in the
modern world the empires of history. To them
Imperialism meant to extend and preserve the
principles of justice, liberty, and peace, which
they believed were inherent in British institutions and more nearly attainable under
monarchical than under republican forms.

Minds influential in the Colonial Office and
elsewhere saw in this only a flamboyant
patriotism. The Duke of Newcastle, when
colonial secretary, had not shared the desire
for separation, and he found it hard to believe that any one charged with colonial administration wished it. He had written to
Palmerston in 1861 :

You speak of some supposed theoretical
gentlemen in the colonial office who wish

to get rid of all colonies as soon as possible. I can only say that if there are such they have never ventured to open their opinion to me. If they did so on grounds of peaceful separation, I should differ from them so long as colonies can be retained by bonds of mutual sympathy and mutual obligation ; but I would meet their views with indignation if they could suggest disruption by the act of any other, and that a hostile, Power.

The duke was not intimate with his official subordinates, or he would have known that Palmerston's description exactly fitted the permanent under-secretary at the Colonial Office. Sir Frederic Rogers (who later became Lord Blachford) filled that post from 1860 to 1871. He was therefore in office during the Confederation period. He left on record his ideas of the future of the Empire :

I had always believed—and the belief has so confirmed and consolidated itself that I can hardly realize the possibility of any one seriously thinking the contrary— that the destiny of our colonies is independence ; and that in this view, the function of the Colonial Office is to secure that our connexion, while it lasts, shall be as profitable to both parties, and our separation, when it comes, as amicable as possible. This opinion is founded first on the general principle that a spirited nation (and a colony becomes a nation) will not submit to be governed in its internal affairs by a distant government, and that nations geographically remote have no such common interests as will bind them permanently together in foreign policy with all its details and mutations.

In other words, Sir Frederic was a painstaking honourable official without a shred of imagination. He typifies the sort of influence which the delegates had to encounter.

The conference consisted of sixteen members, six from Canada and ten from the Maritime Provinces. The Canadians were Macdonald, Cartier, Galt, McDougall, Howland, and Langevin. From Nova Scotia came Tupper, Henry, Ritchie, McCully, and Archibald; while New Brunswick was represented by Tilley, Johnston, Mitchell, Fisher, and Wilmot. They selected John A. Macdonald as chairman. The resignation of Brown had left Macdonald the leader of the movement, and the nominal

Canadian prime minister, Sir Narcisse Belleau, was not even a delegate. The impression Macdonald made in London is thus recorded by Sir Frederic Rogers in language which gives us an insight into the working of the conference:

> They held many meetings, at which I was always present. Lord Carnarvon [the colonial secretary] was in the chair, and I was rather disappointed in his power of presidency. Macdonald was the ruling genius and spokesman, and I was very greatly struck by his power of management and adroitness. The French delegates were keenly on the watch for anything which weakened their securities; on the contrary, the Nova Scotia and New Brunswick delegates were very jealous of concessions to the *arriérée* province; while one main stipulation in favour of the French was open to constitutional objections on the part of the Home Government. Macdonald had to argue the question with the Home Government on a point on which the slightest divergence from the narrow line already agreed upon in Canada was watched for—here by the French and

there by the English—as eager dogs watch a rat hole ; a snap on one side might have provoked a snap on the other and put an end to the concord. He stated and argued the case with cool ready fluency, while at the same time you saw that every word was measured, and that while he was making for a point ahead, he was never for a moment unconscious of any of the rocks among which he had to steer.

The preliminaries had all been settled before the meetings with the colonial secretary. The gathering was smaller in numbers than the Quebec Conference, and the experience of two years had not been lost. We hear no more of deadlocks or of the danger of breaking up. There was frank discussion on any point that required reconsideration, but the delegates decided to adhere to the Quebec resolutions as far as possible. For the Liberal ministers from Upper Canada, Howland and McDougall, this was the safest course to pursue, because they knew that George Brown had put his hand and seal upon the basis adopted at Quebec and would bitterly resent any substantial departure from it. This was also the view of the representatives of Lower Canada. The mari-

THE FRAMING OF THE BILL 125

time delegates wanted better financial terms if such could be secured, but beyond this were content with the accepted outline of the constitution.

The delegates were careful to make plain their belief that the union was to cement and not to weaken the Imperial tie. At Quebec they had agreed upon a motion in these terms :

> That in framing a constitution for the general government, the conference, with a view to the perpetuation of our connection with the Mother Country and to the promotion of the best interests of the people of these provinces, desire to follow the model of the British constitution, so far as our circumstances will permit.

The saving clause at the close was a frank admission that a federal system could not be an exact copy of the British model with its one sovereign parliament charged with the whole power of the nation. But the delegates were determined to express the idea in some form ; and this led to the words in the preamble of the British North America Act declaring ' a constitution similar in principle to that of the United Kingdom.' To this writers of note have objected. Professor Dicey has complained of the ' official mendacity ' involved in the statement. ' If preambles were intended to express the truth,' he said, ' for the word *Kingdom* ought to have been substituted *States*, since it is clear that the constitution of the Dominion is modelled on that of the United States.' It is, however, equally clear what the framers of the Act intended to convey. If they offended against the precise canons of constitutional theory, they effected a political object of greater consequence. The Canadian constitution, in their opinion, was British in principle for at least three reasons : because it provided for responsible government in both the general and local legislatures ; because, unlike the system in the United States, the executive and legislative functions were not divorced ; and because this enabled Canada to incorporate the traditions and conventions of the British constitution which bring the executive immediately under control of the popular wish as expressed through parliament. Furthermore, the principle of defining the jurisdictions of the provinces, while the residue of power was left to the federal parliament, marked another wide distinction between Canada and the Republic. A federation it had to be, but a federation designed in the narrowest sense. In theory Canada is a dependent and subordinate country, since its constitution was conferred by an Act of the Imperial parliament, but in practice it is a self-governing state in the fullest degree. This anomaly, so fortunate in its results, is no greater than the maintenance in theory of royal prerogatives which are never exercised.

It was intended that the name of the new state should be left to the selection of the Queen, and this was provided for in the first draft of the bill. But the proposal was soon dropped. It revived the memory of the regrettable incident of 1858 when the Queen had, by request, selected Ottawa as the Canadian capital and her decision had been condemned by a vote of the legislature. The press had discussed a suitable name long before the London delegates assembled. Some favoured New Britain, while others preferred Laurentia or Britannia. If the maritime union had been effected, the name of that division would probably have been Acadia, and this name was suggested for the larger union. Other ideas were merely fantastic, such as Cabotia, Columbia, Canadia, and Ursalia. The decision that Canada should give up its name to the new Confederation and that Upper and Lower Canada should find new names for themselves was undoubtedly a happy conclusion to the discussion. It was desired to call the Confederation the Kingdom of Canada, and thus fix the monarchical basis of the constitution. The French were especially attached to this idea. The word Kingdom appeared in an early draft of the bill as it came from the conference. But it was vetoed by the foreign secretary, Lord Stanley,[1] who thought that the republican sensibilities of the United States would be wounded. This preposterous notion serves to indicate the inability of the controlling minds of the period to grasp the true nature of the change. Finally, the word ' Dominion' was decided upon. Why a term was selected which is so difficult to render in the French language (*La Puissance* is the translation employed) is not easy of comprehension. There is a story, probably invented, that when ' Dominion' was under consideration, a member of the conference, well versed in the Scriptures, found a verse which, as a piece of descriptive prophecy, at once clinched the matter : ' And his dominion shall be from

[1] He became Lord Derby in 1869 and bore this title in 1889 when Sir John Macdonald related the incident.

sea even to sea, and from the river even to the
ends of the earth.' [1]

The knotty question of the second chamber,
supposed to have been solved at Quebec, came
up again. The notes of the discussion [2] are
as interesting as the surviving notes of the
Quebec Conference. Some of the difficulties
since experienced were foreseen. But no one
appears to have realized that the Senate would
become the citadel of a defeated party, until
sufficient vacancies by death should occur to
transform it into the obedient instrument of
the government of the day. No one foresaw,
in truth, that the Senate would consider
measures chiefly on party grounds, and would
fail to demonstrate the usefulness of a second
chamber by industry and capacity in revising
hasty legislation. The delegates actually believed that equality of representation between
the three divisions, Upper Canada, Lower
Canada, and the Maritime Provinces, would
make the Senate a bulwark of protection to
individual provinces. In this character it
has never shone.[3] Its chief value has been as

[1] Zechariah ix 10.
[2] Sir Joseph Pope's *Confederation Documents.*
[3] The recent increase in the number of western senators
modifies this feature.

a reservoir of party patronage. The opinions of several of the delegates are prophetical :

HENRY (Nova Scotia)—I oppose the limitation of number. We want a complete work. Do you wish to stereotype an upper branch irresponsible both to the crown and the people ? A third body interposed unaccountable to the other two. The crown unable to add to their number. The people unable to remove them. Suppose a general election results in the election of a large majority in the Lower House favourable to a measure, but the legislative council prevents it from becoming law. The crown should possess some power of enlargement.

FISHER (New Brunswick)—The prerogative of the crown has been only occasionally used and always for good. This new fangled thing now introduced, seventy-two oligarchs, will introduce trouble. I advocate the principle of the power of the crown to appoint additional members in case of emergency.

HOWLAND (Upper Canada)—My remedy would be to limit the period of service and vest the appointment in the local legislatures. Now, it is an anomaly. It won't work and cannot be continued. You cannot give the crown an unlimited power to appoint.

One result of the views exchanged is found in the twenty-sixth section of the Act. This gives the sovereign, acting of course on the advice of his ministers and at the request of the Canadian government, the right to add

three or six members to the Senate, selected
equally from the three divisions mentioned
above. These additional members are not to
be a permanent increase of the Senate, because
vacancies occurring thereafter are not to be
filled until the normal number is restored.
Once only has it been sought to invoke the
power of this section. In 1873, when the
first Liberal ministry after Confederation was
formed, the prime minister, Alexander Mackenzie, finding himself faced by a hostile
majority in the Senate, asked the Queen to add
six members to the Senate 'in the public interests.' The request was refused. The colonial
secretary, Lord Kimberley, held that the power
was intended solely to bring the two Houses
into accord when an actual collision of opinion
took place of so serious and permanent a kind
that the government could not be carried on
without the intervention of the sovereign as
prescribed in this section. The Conservative
majority in the Senate highly approved of
this decision, and expressed its appreciation
in a series of resolutions which are a fine display of unconscious humour.

Not the least important of the changes in
the scheme adopted at London was that relating to the educational privileges of minori-

ties. This is embodied in the famous ninety-third section of the Act, and originated in a desire to protect the Protestant minority in Lower Canada. Its champion was Galt. An understanding existed that the Canadian parliament would enact the necessary guarantees before Canada entered the union. But the proposal, when brought before the House in 1866, was so expressed as to apply to the schools of both the Protestant minority in Lower Canada and the Catholic minority in Upper Canada. This led to disturbing debates and was withdrawn. No substitute being offered, Galt, deeming himself pledged to his co-religionists, at once resigned his place in the Cabinet and stated his reasons temperately in parliament. Although no longer a minister, he was selected as one of the London delegates, partly because of the prominent part taken by him in the cause of Confederation and partly in order that the anxieties of the Lower Canada minority might be allayed. Galt's conduct throughout was entirely worthy of him. That he was an enlightened man the memoranda of the London proceedings prove, for there is a provision in his handwriting showing his desire to extend to all minorities the protection he claimed for the Lower

Canada Protestants. The clause drawn by him differs in its phraseology from the wording in the Act and is as follows:

> And in any province where a system of separation or dissentient schools by law obtains, or where the local legislature may adopt a system of separate or dissentient schools, an appeal shall lie to the governor in council of the general government from the acts and decisions of the local authorities which may affect the rights or privileges of the Protestant or Catholic minority in the matter of education. And the general parliament shall have power in the last resort to legislate on the subject.[1]

The bill passed through parliament without encountering any serious opposition. Lord Carnarvon's introductory speech in the House of Lords was an adequate, although not an eloquent, presentation of the subject. His closing words were impressive:

> We are laying the foundation of a great State—perhaps one which at a future day

[1] *Confederation Documents*, p. 112. Mr Justice Day of Montreal, an English Protestant enjoying the confidence of the French, is believed to have had a hand in framing the Galt policy on this subject.

may even overshadow this country. But, come what may, we shall rejoice that we have shown neither indifference to their wishes nor jealousy of their aspirations, but that we honestly and sincerely, to the utmost of our power and knowledge, fostered their growth, recognizing in it the conditions of our own greatness. We are in this measure setting the crown to the free institutions which more than a quarter of a century ago we gave them, and therein we remove, as I firmly believe, all possibilities of future jealousy or misunderstanding.

No grave objections were raised in either the Lords or the Commons. In fact, the criticisms were of a mild character. No division was taken at any stage. In the House of Commons, Mr Adderley, the under-secretary for the Colonies, who was in charge of the measure, found a cordial supporter, instead of a critic, in Mr Cardwell, the former colonial secretary, so that the bill was carried through with ease and celerity. John Bright's speech reflected the anti-Imperial spirit of the time. ' I want the population of these provinces,' he said, ' to do that which they believe to be the best for their own interests—remain with this country if they like, in the most friendly manner, or become independent states if they like. If they should prefer to unite themselves with the United States, I should not complain even of that.'

The strenuous protests made by Joseph Howe and the Nova Scotian opponents of Confederation were not unnoticed. It was claimed by one or two speakers that the electors of that province should be allowed to pronounce upon the measure, but this evoked no support, and the wishes of all the provinces were considered to have been sufficiently consulted. The argument for further delay failed to enlist any active sympathy ; and the wish of the delegates that no material alteration be made in the bill, as it was a compromise based upon a carefully arranged agreement, was respected. The constitution was thus the creation of the colonial statesmen themselves, and not of the Imperial government or parliament.

That so important a step in the colonial policy of the Empire should have been received at London in a passive and indifferent spirit has often been the subject of complaint. When the Australian Commonwealth came into existence, the event was marked by more ceremony and signalized by greater impressiveness. But another phase of the question should be kept in mind. The British North America Act contained the promise of the vast Dominion which exists to-day, but not the reality. The measure dealt with the union of the four provinces only. The Confederation, as we have it, was still incomplete. When the royal proclamation was issued on the 10th of May bringing the new Dominion into being on July 1, 1867, much remained to be done. The constitution must be put to the test of practical experience ; and the task of extending the Dominion across the continent must be undertaken. Upon the first government of Canada, in truth, would rest a duty as arduous as ever fell to the lot of statesmen. They had in their hands a half-finished structure, and might, conceivably, fail in completing it.

CHAPTER XII

THE FIRST DOMINION MINISTRY

BEFORE the delegates left London the governor-general privately invited John A. Macdonald to form the first ministry of the Dominion. A month later the same offer was made more formally in writing :

I entrust this duty to you as the individual selected for their chairman and spokesman by the unanimous vote of the delegates when they were in England, and I adopt this test for my guidance in consequence of the impossibility, under the circumstances, of ascertaining, in the ordinary constitutional manner, who possesses the confidence of a Parliament which does not yet exist. In authorizing you to undertake the duty of forming an administration for the Dominion of Canada, I desire to express my strong opinion that, in future, it shall be distinctly understood that the position of first minister shall be

held by *one* person, who shall be responsible
to the Governor-General for the appointment of the other ministers, and that the
system of dual first ministers, which has
hitherto prevailed, shall be put an end
to.[1]

The selection of Macdonald was inevitable.
When George Brown by his action in 1864
made Confederation possible and entered a
Cabinet where his great rival was the commanding influence, he must have foreseen that,
in the event of the cause succeeding, his own
chances of inaugurating the new state as its
chief figure were not good. And by leaving
the coalition abruptly before union was accomplished he had put himself entirely out of the
running. In a group of able men which included several potential prime ministers Macdonald had advanced to the first place by
reason of gifts precisely suited to the demands
of the hour. Lord Monck's choice was therefore justified. Nor was the resolve to abolish
the awkward and indefensible system of a dual
premiership less open to question. It may
have given pain to Cartier, but it was a wise
and necessary decision.

[1] *Memoirs*, vol. i, p. 319.

Lord Monck, however, does not rank high in the list of talented men who have filled the office of governor-general. The post had gone a-begging when he accepted it in 1861. It had been offered to and refused by Lord Wodehouse, a former viceroy of Ireland; Lord Harris, once governor of Madras and a contemporary of Elgin; Lord Eversley, who had been speaker of the House of Commons; and the Duke of Buckingham. Lord Monck had scarcely arrived in Canada when the *Trent* Affair occurred. Later on the St Albans Raid intensified the bitter feelings between Great Britain and the United States. On both occasions he performed his duties as an Imperial officer judiciously and well. But his relations with Canadian affairs were not so happy. He became dissatisfied with the political conditions as he found them; and his petulance over the slow progress of Confederation led him to threaten resignation. He contrived, moreover, to incur much personal unpopularity, which found vent, during the first session of the Dominion parliament, in a measure to reduce the salary of the governor-general from £10,000 to $32,000. That this unparalleled action was, in part, directed at Lord Monck is shown in the determination to put the reduction in force at once. The home authorities, however, disallowed the bill. In his speech in the House of Lords on the British North America Act, Monck failed to rise to the occasion, owing to a sympathy with the views of the Manchester School. To remain long enough in Canada to preside over the new Dominion had been his own wish. But it does not appear that he utilized his opportunities to marked advantage.

A unique political situation confronted Macdonald. It was natural to suppose that, as the federation leaders belonged to both parties, the first Cabinet should be composed of representative men of both. This was the line Macdonald proposed to take. By this policy a strong national party, with larger aims, would arise, and the old prejudices and issues would be swept away. This statesmanlike conception involved certain embarrassments, because the number of ambitious men looking for Cabinet appointments would be increased and the expectations of faithful Conservative supporters must suffer disappointment. These problems, however, were not new to Macdonald. He had faced similar dangers before, and his skill in handling them was equal to his experience.

Meanwhile, Brown set himself to prevent a plan which would detach a section of the Liberals from their former associates and permanently range them under a Conservative leader. He cannot be blamed for this. Confederation being now a fact, he considered himself under no obligation to continue an alliance proposed for a special object. Although Macdonald might be able to enlist the support of some maritime Liberals, Brown strove to reunite his party in Ontario and present a solid phalanx to the enemy.

A Liberal convention met in Toronto on the 27th and 28th of June 1867. There was a good attendance, and impassioned appeals were made to men of the party throughout the province to join in opposing any ministry which Macdonald might form. It was generally understood that the three Liberal ministers—Howland, McDougall, and Blair—were to continue in the government, which would be renewed as a coalition with a certain degree of Liberal support in the House. To strict party men this was obnoxious. George Brown denounced any further coalition of parties :

If, sir, there is any large number of men in this assembly who will record their votes this night in favour of the degradation of the public men of that party [the Liberals] by joining a coalition, I neither want to be a leader nor a humble member of that party. [Cheers.] If that is the reward you intend to give us all for our services, I scorn connection with you. [Immense cheering.] Go into the same government with Mr John A. Macdonald ! [Cries of never ! never !] Sir, I understood what degradation it was to be compelled to adopt that step by the necessities of the case, by the feeling that the interests of my country were at stake, which alone induced me ever to put my foot into that government ; and glad was I when I got out of it. None ever went into a government with such sore hearts as did two out of the three who entered it on behalf of the Reform party—I cannot speak for the third. It was the happiest day of my life when I got out of the concern. [Cheers.]

These were warm words, designed to rally a divided party. In due time the tireless energy of the speaker and his friends reawakened the fighting strength of their followers. For the moment, however, a considerable number of

Liberals were disposed to give the new conditions a trial. Howland and McDougall were invited to address the convention, and they put their case in temperate and dignified language. Howland pointed out that in the new ministry there would be several Liberals from the lower provinces, and these men had requested their Ontario friends not to leave them. McDougall's address was especially apt and convincing :

> We think that the work of coalition is not done, but only begun. We think that British Columbia should be brought into the confederacy, that the great northwestern territory should be brought in, that Prince Edward Island and Newfoundland should be brought in. I say that the negotiations of the terms upon which these provinces are to be brought in are important, and that it is as necessary that the government in power should not be obliged to fight from day to day for its political existence, as when Confederation was carried up to the point we have now reached. . . . I think the coalition ought not to cease until the work begun under Mr Brown's auspices is ended.

It was evident from these remarks that the arguments—what his critics called the blandishments—of Macdonald had prevailed.

The first Cabinet, which was announced on July 1, began on a non-party basis. This commended it to moderate men generally. But the task of getting it together had been herculean. To secure a ministry representative of all parts of the country seemed a reasonable policy at the beginning. With time this has grown into an unwritten convention of the constitution which cannot be ignored. In 1867 the Cabinet representation had to be determined by geography, race, creed, and party. None but an old parliamentary hand could have made the attempt successfully. Ontario claimed and was assigned five ministers, Quebec four, and the Maritime Provinces four. So much for geography. Then came race and creed. It was found necessary to give the Irish Catholics and the English minority in Quebec each a minister. The French demanded and were granted three ministers. Finally, the fusion of parties imposed another difficulty upon the cabinet-maker. He could not find room for all the really deserving. There were thirteen ministers—too many,

thought Brown and the *Globe*—and of these
six were Liberal and six Conservative, while
Kenny of Nova Scotia had once been a
Liberal but had lately acted with the Tupper
party. The surprises were the absence of the
names of McGee and Tupper from the list. To
have selected McGee as the Irish Catholic
minister meant five representatives for Quebec,
and Ontario would not consent. This threatened a deadlock, and Macdonald was about to
advise the governor-general to send for George
Brown, when McGee and Tupper, with a disinterested generosity rare in politics, waived
their claims, and Edward Kenny became the
Irish representative and second minister from
Nova Scotia. The first administration was
thus constituted :

JOHN A. MACDONALD, Prime Minister and Minister
of Justice.
GEORGE E. CARTIER, Minister of Militia and
Defence.
S. LEONARD TILLEY, Minister of Customs.
ALEXANDER T. GALT, Minister of Finance.
WILLIAM McDOUGALL, Minister of Public Works.
WILLIAM P. HOWLAND, Minister of Inland Revenue.
ADAMS G. ARCHIBALD, Secretary of State for the
Provinces.
A. J. FERGUSSON BLAIR, President of the Privy
Council.

F.O.C.   K

PETER MITCHELL, Minister of Marine and Fisheries.
ALEXANDER CAMPBELL, Postmaster-General.
JEAN C. CHAPAIS, Minister of Agriculture.
HECTOR L. LANGEVIN, Secretary of State of Canada.
EDWARD KENNY, Receiver-General.

The two men who had stepped aside in order that a ministry might be formed under Macdonald were actuated partly by personal regard for their leader. It was not a small sacrifice. Macdonald wrote to McGee:

> The difficulties of adjusting the representation in the Cabinet from the several provinces were great and embarrassing. Your disinterested and patriotic conduct—and I speak of Tupper as well as yourself—had certainly the effect of removing those difficulties. Still, I think you should have first consulted me. However, the thing is done and can't be undone for the present; but I am very sure that at a very early day your valuable services will be sought for by the government.

McGee was to have retired from political life and to have received the appointment of commissioner of patents at $3200 a year, a sinecure which would have enabled him to pursue his literary work. His assassination in the early morning of April 7, 1868, on returning to his lodging after a late session of the House, is one of the most tragic episodes in the annals of Canada.

The ministers having been sworn of the Privy Council, Lord Monck announced that Her Majesty had been pleased to confer upon the new prime minister the rank of Knight Commander of the Bath, and upon Cartier, Galt, Tilley, Tupper, Howland, and McDougall the companionship of the same order. No previous intimation had been given to any of them. Cartier and Galt, deeming the recognition of their services inadequate, declined to receive it. This incident is only worthy of mention because it tended to disturb the personal relations of men who should have acted in complete harmony at a time of national importance. No Imperial honours had been conferred in Canada since 1860, and it was unfortunate that the advice tendered the crown on this historic occasion should have been open to criticism and have engendered ill feeling. Cartier thought that his race had been affronted in his person, and his reasons for protest were political. He told his colleagues: 'Personally I care nothing for honours, but as a representative of one of the two great provinces in Confederation I have a position to maintain, and I shall not accept the honour. I regret that such an action is necessary, because it may be construed as an insult to Her Majesty. I feel aggrieved that I should not have been notified in advance, so that I should not now have to refuse, but I shall write to Her Majesty myself explaining the reasons for my refusing the honour.' [1] The error was soon rectified and Cartier was made a baronet. A number of persons, including Charles Tupper and Edward Watkin, a member of the Imperial parliament, interested themselves in the matter, pointing out to the London authorities the unwisdom of bestowing titles without due regard to the Imperial services of the recipients. The reputations of Galt and Cartier as serious statesmen were not enhanced. Explain it as we may, there is a flavour of absurdity about their proceedings. Galt was offered a knighthood in 1869, and would not accept until the Imperial government had been made aware of his views upon the ultimate destiny of Canada. In a letter to the governor-general he thus placed himself on record :

[1] *Sir George Etienne Cartier, Bart., His Life and Times*, by John Boyd. Toronto, 1914.

I regard the confederation of the British North American Provinces as a measure which must ultimately lead to their separation from Great Britain. The present connection is undoubtedly an embarrassment to Great Britain in her relations to the United States and a source of uneasiness to the Dominion, owing to the insecurity which is felt to exist from the possibility of a rupture between the two nations. It cannot be the policy of England, and is certainly not the desire of the people here, to become annexed to the United States; but I believe the best, and indeed the only way to prevent this, is to teach the Canadian people to look forward to an independent existence as a nation in the future as desirable and possible. Unless such a spirit be cultivated, the idea will become engrained in the public mind, that failing the connection with Great Britain annexation must ensue.

Galt went on to state that he hoped separation would be postponed as long as possible. The reply of the secretary of state, Lord Granville, was private, but it appears to have been in effect a declaration that Galt could hold any views he pleased about the future of the Empire. He accepted the K.C.M.G. and worthily wore it to the end of an honourable and public-spirited career. Thus was vindicated the freedom of speech which is the birthright of every British subject. But Galt, in exercising it, showed lack of stability and a tendency to take an erratic course, which crippled his influence in the young state he had done so much to found.

It was an enormous burden of duty which now fell upon the executive. The whole machinery of state required recasting. The uncertainties of a situation wherein party bonds sat lightly and diversities of opinion lingered, taxed all the resources of the leader of the government. Although different views are held as to the particular stage in his long career in which the remarkable qualities of Sir John Macdonald displayed themselves most conspicuously, the first five years of the union may well be regarded by future historians as the period when his patience, tenacity, and adroitness were especially in evidence.

The provincial governments had to be constituted ; and in Ontario Macdonald scored again by persuading Sandfield Macdonald to form a coalition ministry in which party lines were effaced and the policy of coalition was defended by an erstwhile Liberal leader. Sandfield Macdonald was a man of talent and integrity. His attitude of mind was rather that of an oppositionist, upon whom the functions of independent critic sat more easily than the compromises and discipline entailed by party leadership. He bore restraint with impatience, and if his affiliations had always been with the Liberals, it was not because his sympathies were radical and progressive.[1] In the Liberal caucus of 1864 he had moved the resolution requesting George Brown to enter the coalition government, without recognizing, apparently, that he thereby incurred an obligation himself to support federation. Both in the Ontario legislature, where he was loth to follow any course but his own, and in the Dominion parliament, where he ostentatiously

[1] Sir James Whitney, prime minister of Ontario from 1905 to 1914, who was a young student in Sandfield Macdonald's law office in Cornwall and shared his political confidence, assured the present writer that Ontario's first prime minister was not a Liberal in the real sense, his instincts and point of view being essentially Conservative. After Robert Baldwin's retirement Sandfield Macdonald's natural course would have been an alliance with the progressive Conservatives under John A. Macdonald, but his antipathy to acknowledging any leader kept him aloof. His laconic telegram in reply to John A. Macdonald's offer of cabinet office is characteristic: ' No go !'

sat on an Opposition bench, he presented a shining example of that type of mind which lacks the capacity for unity and co-operation with others. He illustrated, too, one of the difficult features of Macdonald's problem—the absence of unity among the public men of the time—a condition which complicated, if it did not retard, the formation of a homogeneous national sentiment.[1]

The general elections were impending, and everything turned upon the verdict of the country. The first elections for the House of Commons took place during the months of August and September, the practice of holding elections all on one day having not yet come into vogue. The three provinces of Ontario, Quebec, and New Brunswick sustained the government by large majorities. But in Nova Scotia the agitation against the union swept the province. Tupper was the only Conservative elected. His victory was the more notable in that he defeated William Annand, the chief lieutenant of Howe and afterwards the leader of the repeal movement. Adams Archibald, the secretary of state, was

[1] A conspicuous case in point is the entire want of sympathy between Brown and Galt, men of similar type, whose opinions on several questions coincided.

defeated in Colchester by A. W. McLelan, and Henry, another member of the Quebec Conference, was rejected in Antigonish. In Ontario there were losses. George Brown was defeated in South Ontario by a few votes, and did not again sit in parliament until he was appointed to the Senate in 1874. In the early years of the Dominion a member might sit both in the House of Commons and in the legislature of his province. So it was that at this election Edward Blake was returned from South Bruce to the Ontario legislature and from West Durham to the House of Commons. Other members who occupied seats in both bodies were Sandfield Macdonald, John Carling, Alexander Mackenzie, and E. B. Wood. Cartier's success in Quebec left his opponents only fifteen seats out of sixty-five. The stars in their courses fought for the government; and had it not been for Nova Scotia, where the victorious and hostile forces were pledged to repeal, the consolidation of the Dominion could have gone forward without hindrance.

To deal with ' that pestilent fellow Howe,' to use Macdonald's phrase, was a first charge upon the energies of the government. The history of the repeal movement in Nova Scotia, with all its incidents and sidelights, has yet to be written. It was but one of the disintegrating forces which Macdonald found so hard to cope with, that in a moment of discouragement he seriously thought of withdrawing from the government and letting others carry it on. A large portion of the year 1868 was occupied with the effort to reconcile the Nova Scotians. Instead of abating, the anti-confederate feeling in that province grew more bitter. A delegation headed by Howe and Annand went to England to demand repeal from the Imperial authorities. To counteract this move the Dominion government sent Charles Tupper to present the other side of the case. None of the passages in his political life reflect more credit upon him than his diplomacy upon this occasion. He had already declined, as we have seen, a seat in the Cabinet. Later, he had further strengthened his reputation by refusing the lucrative office of chairman of the commission to build the Intercolonial Railway. This fresh display of independence enabled him to meet the repeal delegates on ground as patriotic as their own, for it had shown that in this crisis they were not the only Nova Scotians who wanted nothing for themselves.

Tupper's first step on reaching London was to call on Howe. ' I said to him,' writes Tupper, ' I will not insult you by suggesting that you should fail to undertake the mission that brought you here. When you find out, however, that the Government and the Imperial Parliament are overwhelmingly against you, it is important for you to consider the next step.' [1] This was to put the finger upon the weakest spot in Howe's armour. After his mission had failed and the Imperial authorities had refused to allow the union to be broken up, as they most assuredly would, what could Howe and his friends do next ? A revolution was unthinkable. A province ' on strike ' would have no adequate means of raising a revenue, and a government lacking the power of taxation soon ceases to exist. The extremists talked Annexation ; but in this they counted without Howe and the loyal province of Nova Scotia. The movement, noisy and formidable as it appeared, was foredoomed to failure. All this Tupper put to Joseph Howe ; and when Tupper proposed that Howe should enter the Dominion Cabinet, not as his docile follower but as his leader, it

[1] *Recollections of Sixty Years in Canada*, by the Rt Hon. Sir Charles Tupper, Bart.

can readily be believed that he was ' completely staggered.'

True to Tupper's forecast, and due in part, at least, to his powerful advocacy of the cause of union, the home government stood firm against the cry from Nova Scotia. The delegates and their opponents returned home. Then the rapid development of events compelled Howe to face the issue : when legal and constitutional methods were exhausted without avail, what then ? The crisis came. Howe was obliged to break with his associates, some of whom were preaching sedition, and to take a stand more in accordance with his real convictions and his Imperial sentiments. Early in August 1868 Sir John Macdonald went to Halifax and met the leading malcontents. ' They have got the idea into their heads,' wrote Howe in a private letter, ' that you are a sort of wizard that, having beguiled Brown, McDougall, Tupper, etc., to destruction, is about to do the same kind of office to me.' Howe was not beguiled, but a master of tactics showed him the means by which Nova Scotia could be kept in the union ; the way was paved for a final settlement ; and a few months later Howe joined the Dominion government.

Long after Joseph Howe had passed to his

rest, echoes of the repeal agitation were heard in Nova Scotia ; and it was frequently asserted that the question of union should have been submitted to a vote of the people. Such a course, owing to the circumstances already narrated, was impracticable and would have been fatal to Confederation. But the pacification of the province was a great feat of statesmanship ; for to maintain the young Dominion intact was essential to its further extension.

CHAPTER XIII

FROM SEA TO SEA

THE extension of the Dominion to the Pacific ocean had been discussed at the Quebec Conference. Some of the maritime delegates, however, thought they had no authority to discuss the acquisition of territory beyond the boundaries of the provinces; and George Brown, one of the strongest advocates of western extension, conceded that the inclusion of British Columbia and Vancouver Island in the scheme of union was ' rather an extreme proposition.' But the Canadian leaders never lost sight of the intervening regions of Rupert's Land and the North-West Territory. They foresaw the danger of the rich prairie lands falling under foreign control, and entertained no doubts as to the necessity of terminating in favour of Canada the hold of the Hudson's Bay Company over these regions.

In 1857 the select committee of the Imperial House of Commons, mentioned in a preceding

chapter, had believed it ' essential to meet the
just and reasonable wishes of Canada to be
enabled to annex to her territory such portion
of the land in her neighbourhood as may be
available to her for the purposes of settlement.'
The districts on the Red River and on the
Saskatchewan were considered as likely to be
desired ; and, as a condition of occupation,
Canada should open up and maintain communication and provide for local administration. The committee thought that if Canada
were unwilling to take over the Red River
country at an early date some temporary
means of government might be devised. Nothing, however, had come of the suggestion.
Had it been carried out, and a crown colony
created, comprising the territory which is now
the province of Manitoba, the Dominion would
have been saved a disagreeable and humiliat-
ing episode, as well as political complications
which shook the young state to its foundations.
This was the trouble known to history as the
Red River Rebellion. As an armed insurrec-
tion it was only a flash in the pan. But it
awoke passions in Ontario and Quebec, and
revived all those dissensions, racial and religious, which the union had lulled into a sem-
blance of harmony.

One of the first steps taken by parliament in the autumn of 1867 was the adoption of an address to the Queen, moved by William McDougall, asking that Rupert's Land and the North-West Territory be united with Canada. Two members of the government, Cartier and McDougall, went to England to negotiate for the extinction of the rights of the Hudson's Bay Company. After months of delay, caused partly by the serious illness of McDougall, it was agreed that the company should receive £300,000, one-twentieth of the lands lying within the Fertile Belt, and 45,000 acres adjacent to its trading-posts. The Canadian parliament formally accepted the bargain, and the deed of surrender provided that the change of rule should come into force on December 1, 1869.

It was no mean ambition of William McDougall to be the first Canadian administrator of this vast region with its illimitable prospects ; a man of talent, experience, and breadth of view, such as McDougall was, might reasonably hope there to carve out a great career for himself and do the state some service. He was appointed on September 26, 1869, lieutenant-governor of the ' North-West Territory '—an indefinite term meant appar-

ently to cover the whole western country—
and left at once for his post. He appears to
have been quite in the dark concerning the
perilous nature of the mission. At any rate,
he could not foresee that, far from bringing
him distinction, the task would shortly end,
as Sir John Macdonald described it, in an in-
glorious fiasco.

At this time, it should be remembered, the
actual conditions in the West were but vaguely
known in Canada. Efforts towards communication and exploration, it is true, had begun
as early as 1857, when Simon Dawson made
surveys for a road from Fort William and
Professor Henry Youle Hind undertook his
famous journey to the plains for scientific and
general observation. A number of adventurous Canadians had gone out to settle on the
plains. There was a newspaper at Fort Garry
—the *Nor' Wester*—the pioneer newspaper of
the country—which had been started by Mr
William Buckingham and a colleague in 1859.
But even in official circles the community to
which Governor McDougall went to introduce
authority was very imperfectly understood.

The Red River Settlement in 1869 contained
about twelve thousand inhabitants. The
English-speaking portion of the population

consisted of heterogeneous groups without unity among them for any public purpose. Some were descendants or survivors of Lord Selkirk's settlers who had come out half a century before; others were servants of the Hudson's Bay Company, both retired and active; a third group were the Canadians; while a fourth was made up of a small though noisy body of Americans. Outnumbering the English, and united under leaders of their own race, the French and French half-breeds dwelt chiefly on the east bank of the Red River, south of Fort Garry. These half-breeds, or Métis, were a hardy race, who subsisted by hunting rather than by farming, and who were trained to the use of arms. They regarded with suspicion the threatened introduction of new political institutions, and were quite content under the paternal sway of the Hudson's Bay Company and under the leadership of their spiritual advisers, Bishop Taché and the priests of the Métis parishes.

The Canadian population numbered about three hundred, with perhaps a hundred adults, and they, conscious that they represented the coming régime, were not disposed to conciliate either the company or the native settlers. It was mooted among the half-breeds that they were to be swamped by the incoming Canadians, and much resentment was aroused among them against the assumption of authority by the Dominion government. To make matters worse, a Canadian surveying party, led by Colonel J. Stoughton Dennis, had begun in the summer of 1869 to make surveys in the Province. This created alarm among the half-breed settlers, whose titles did not rest in any secure legal authority, and who were fearful that they were about to lose their possessions. Thus it came about that they resolved upon making a determined attempt to resist the transfer of the country to Canada.

Underrating the difficulty and impatient of delay, McDougall took the unwise step of issuing a proclamation, from his temporary headquarters at Pembina, assuming control of the territory and calling upon the inhabitants to recognize his authority. He supposed, of course, that the transfer would be made, according to agreement, on December 1, and did not know that the Canadian government had declined to accept it or pay over the purchase-money until assured that peace and good order prevailed. The advices from Ottawa to McDougall were delayed, and he felt himself obliged to act without definite knowledge of the position of affairs.

After months of agitation the Métis under Louis Riel took command of the situation, armed their fighting men, seized Fort Garry, put a number of prominent white residents under arrest, and formed a provisional government. They sent word to the new governor not to enter the country; and when he advanced, with his official party, a short distance over the frontier, he was forcibly compelled by the insurgents to retreat into the United States. The rebels at Fort Garry became extremely menacing. Louis Riel, the central figure in this drama, was a young French half-breed, vain, ambitious, with some ability and the qualities of a demagogue. He had received his education in Lower Canada, and was on intimate terms with the French priests of the settlement. His conduct fifteen years later, when he returned to head another Métis rebellion farther west and paid the penalty on the scaffold, indicates that once embarked on a dangerous course he would be restrained by no one. That he was half, or wholly, insane on either occasion is not credible.

Efforts were now made to negotiate with

the rebels and quiet the disturbance. Delegates went to the West from Canada consisting of Grand Vicar Thibault, Colonel de Salaberry, and Donald A. Smith (afterwards Lord Strathcona). There were exciting scenes ; but the negotiations bore no immediate fruit. It was the depth of winter. The delegates had not come to threaten because they had no force to employ. The rebels had the game in their own hands. Bishop Taché, who was unhappily absent in Rome, was summoned home to arrange a peace on terms which might have left Riel and his associates some of the high stakes for which they were playing, had they not spoiled their own chances by a cruel, vindictive murder.

After the departure of the Canadian delegates and the announcement of Bishop Taché's return, Riel felt his power ebbing away. His provisional government became a thing of shreds and patches, in spite of its large assumptions and its temporary control during the winter when the country was inaccessible. Among the imprisoned whites was Thomas Scott, a young man from Ontario who had been employed in surveying work and who was prominent in resistance to the usurpers. Riel is credited with a threat to shed some blood to prove the reality of his power and to quell opposition. He rearrested a number of whites who had been released under promise of safety. One of them was Scott, charged with insubordination and breaking his parole. He was brought before a revolutionary tribunal resembling a court-martial, and was sentenced to be shot. Even if Riel's lawless tribunal had possessed judicial authority, Scott's conduct in no respect justified a death sentence. He had not been under arms when captured, and he was given no fair opportunity of defending himself. Efforts were made to save him, but Riel refused to show mercy. On March 4, a few days before Bishop Taché arrived at the settlement, Scott was shot by six men, several of them intoxicated, one refusing to prime his rifle, and one discharging a pistol at the victim as he lay moaning on the ground.

When the news of this barbarous murder reached the East, a political crisis was imminent. Scott was an Orangeman; and Catholic priests, it was said, had been closely identified with the rising. This was enough to start an agitation and to give it the character of a race and creed struggle. There existed also a suspicion that a miniature Quebec was to

ALEXANDRE ANTONIN TACHÉ

From a photograph lent by Rev. L. Messier, St Boniface

be set up on the Red River, thus creating a sort of buffer French state between Ontario and the plains. Another cause of discontent was the belief that the government proposed to connive at the assassination of Scott and to allow his murderers to escape punishment. McDougall returned home, mortified by his want of success, and soon resigned his position. He blamed the government for what had occurred, and associated himself with the agitation in Ontario. The organization known as the Canada First party took a hand in the fray. It was composed of a few patriotic and able young men, including W. A. Foster, a Toronto barrister ; Charles Mair, the well-known poet ; John Schultz, who many years later, as Sir John Schultz, became governor of Manitoba, and who with Mair had been imprisoned by Riel and threatened with death; and Colonel George T. Denison, whose distinguished career as the promoter of Imperial unity has since made him famous in Canada and far beyond it.

The circumstances of the time, the distrust between the races and the vacillation of a sorely pressed government, combined to make an awkward situation. The evidence does not show that the Ontario agitators let slip any of their opportunities. The government was compelled to send under Colonel Wolseley an expeditionary force of Imperial troops and Canadian volunteers to nip in the bud the supposed attempt to establish French ascendancy on the Red River. This expedition was completely successful without the firing of a shot. Riel, at the sight of the troops, fled to the United States, and the British flag was raised over Fort Garry. So, in 1870, Manitoba entered the Dominion as a new province, and the adjacent territories were organized under a lieutenant-governor and council directly under federal jurisdiction. Out of them, thirty-five years later, came the provinces of Alberta and Saskatchewan.

But the fruits of the rebellion were evident for years. One result was the defeat in Ontario of Sandfield Macdonald's ministry in 1871. ' I find the country in a sound state,' wrote Sir John Macdonald during the general elections of 1872, ' the only rock ahead being that infernal Scott murder case, about which the Orangemen have quite lost their heads.' [1]

When order was restored the clever miscreant Riel returned to the settlement. By raising a force to aid in quelling a threatened Fenian

[1] *Memoirs*, vol. ii, p. 150.

invasion, he gulled Bishop Taché and the new governor, Adams G. Archibald, and had himself elected to the Dominion parliament. But Riel's crimes were too recent and too gross to be overlooked. His effrontery in taking the oath as a member was followed by his expulsion from the House; and once more he fled the country, only to reappear in the rôle of a rebel on the Saskatchewan in 1884, and, in the following year, to expiate his crimes on the scaffold.

Having carried the Dominion to the foot of the Rocky Mountains, the next step for the government was the acquisition of British Columbia. After the Oregon Treaty of 1846 the British possessions on the Pacific coast lay in three divisions, Vancouver Island, British Columbia, and the Stikeen Territory, all in the domains of the Hudson's Bay Company. In 1863, after the inrush of gold-seekers, the two latter had been united under one government and granted a Legislative Council, partly elective. Vancouver Island already had a legislature with two chambers, one elective. In 1865 Amor DeCosmos, one of the members of the Assembly for Victoria, began the union movement by proposing that Vancouver Island should be joined to British Columbia. There was friction between the two colonies, largely on commercial grounds. A tariff enacted by the colony on the mainland proved injurious to the island merchants who flourished under a free port. So in 1866 the Imperial parliament passed an Act uniting the two colonies. Despite the isolation of the Pacific coast settlements from the British colonies across the continent on the Atlantic, the Confederation movement had not passed unnoticed in the Far West; and in March 1867 the Legislative Council of British Columbia adopted a resolution requesting Governor Seymour to take measures to secure the admission of British Columbia into the Dominion ' on fair and equitable terms.' In transmitting the resolution to the home authorities the governor candidly pointed out the difficulties. He was not strongly in favour of the policy. The country east of the Rocky Mountains, it should be kept in mind, was still in the hands of the Hudson's Bay Company. An alien population from the United States was increasing in number. Enormous obstacles stood in the way of communication eastward. 'The resolution,' wrote Seymour, ' was the expression of a despondent community longing for change.' However, a public meeting in Victoria held on January

29, 1868, urgently recommended union. A
memorial to the Canadian government declared that the people generally were enthusi-
astic for the change. The leading newspapers
endorsed it. The popularly elected councils
of Victoria and New Westminster were of the
same mind. Opposed to this body of opinion
were the official class and a small party who
desired annexation to the United States. The
terms demanded were the assumption by
Canada of a debt of about $1,500,000, a fixed
annual subsidy, a wagon-road between Lake
Superior and the head of navigation on the
Fraser within two years, local representative
institutions, and representation in the Canadian parliament.

The legislature, despite the alluring prospect
set forth in an address to the Queen moved
by DeCosmos, cautiously adopted an amend-
ment declaring that, while it adhered to its
previous action in endorsing the principle of
union ' to accomplish the consolidation of
British interests and institutions in North
America,' it lacked the knowledge necessary
to define advantageous terms of union. A
convention of delegates met at Yale to express
dissatisfaction with local conditions in British
Columbia and to frame the terms on which

union would be desirable. The Legislative Council, still unconvinced, again declared for delay ; but a dispatch from Lord Granville in August 1869, addressed to the new governor, Anthony Musgrave, who, on the recommendation of Sir John Macdonald, had succeeded Seymour, emphatically endorsed Confederation, leaving open only the question of the terms. The Confederation debate took place in the Legislative Council in 1870. In concluding his speech in favour of the policy, Joseph Trutch, one of the three delegates who afterwards went to Canada to perfect the bargain, said :

> I advocate Confederation because it will secure the continuance of this colony under the British flag and strengthen British interests on this continent, and because it will benefit this community—by lessening taxation and giving increased revenue for local expenditure ; by advancing the political status of the colony ; by securing the practical aid of the Dominion Government . . . ; and by affording, through a railway, the only means of acquiring a permanent population which must come from the east of the Rocky Mountains.

The arrangement made by Canada was a
generous one. It included a promise to begin
within two years and to complete within ten
a railway to the Pacific, thus connecting
British Columbia with the eastern provinces.
The terms were ratified by the people of
British Columbia in the general election of 1870,
and the union went into force on July 20, 1871.
The Dominion now stretched from sea to sea.

Prince Edward Island had fought stoutly
in resistance to the union. For six years it
remained aloof. The fears of a small community, proud of its local rights and conscious
that its place in a federal system could never
be a commanding one, are not to be despised.
At first federation had found eloquent advocates. There could not be, it was pointed out,
any career for men of distinction in a small
sea-girt province cut off completely from the
life and interests of the larger area. But these
arguments failed, as also did proposals of a
more substantial kind. Nova Scotia and New
Brunswick desired greatly to augment the
maritime importance and influence in the
Dominion by the inclusion of the little island
province. During the summer of 1866, while
the delegates from the two maritime provinces

were waiting in London for the arrival of their Canadian colleagues, they made an offer to James C. Pope, prime minister of the Island, who happened to be in London, that the sum of $800,000 should be allowed the Island, in order to extinguish the rights of the absentee land-owners, an incubus that had long caused discontent. The Canadian delegates, at first reluctant, were brought to agree to this proposal. But it was declined, and the same fate overtook better financial terms which Tilley offered in 1869. The Island went its way, but soon found that the capital necessary for internal development was hard to secure and harder still to repay if once obtained. A railway debt was incurred, and financial difficulties arose.

This situation came to the knowledge of Sir John Rose, the first finance minister of Canada, who had gone to reside in London as a partner in the great banking house of Morton, Rose and Co. There is a touch of romance both in the career of Rose and in the fact that it was through his agency that the little province entered the federation. Rose was a Scottish lad who had come to Canada to make his fortune. When a practising barrister in Montreal he had lost his silk gown as Queen's Counsel

for signing the Annexation Manifesto in 1849.
His abilities were of the first order, but his
tastes inclined to law rather than to politics.
The Dominion was in its infancy when his
talents for finance attracted attention abroad
and secured him the handsome offer which
drew him away from Canada and led to his
remarkable success in the money centre of
the world.   But he never lost interest in the
Dominion.   He maintained a close and intimate correspondence with Sir John Macdonald,
and, learning of Prince Edward Island's difficulties, communicated with the Canadian
prime minister.   Thus was the way opened
for negotiations.   Finally a basis of union was
arranged by which the Dominion assumed the
provincial burden and made the Island railway
part of the state system of railways.   Prince
Edward Island joined the union on July 1,
1873, and has contributed its full quota of
brain and energy to the upbuilding of Canada.

Newfoundland definitely rejected union in
the general election of 1869, and only once
since has it shown an inclination to join the
Dominion.   During the financial crisis of 1893
delegates from Newfoundland visited Ottawa
and sought to reach a satisfactory arrange-

ment.   But the opportunity was allowed to pass, and the ancient colony has ever since turned a deaf ear to all suggestions of federation.   But it is still the hope of many that the 'Oldest Colony' will one day acknowledge the hegemony of Canada.

CHAPTER XIV

THE WORK OF THE FATHERS

THE lapse of fifty years should make it possible for us to value the work of the Fathers with due regard for historical truth. Time has thrown into bold relief the essential greatness of their undertaking and has softened the asperities of criticism which seem inseparable from all political movements. A struggle for national unity brings out the stronger qualities of man's nature, but is not a magic remedy for rivalries between the leading minds in the state. On the contrary, it accentuates for the time being the differences of temperament and the clash of individual opinions which accompany a notable effort in nation-making. But distance from the scene and from the men furnishes a truer perspective. The Fathers were not exempt from the defects that mark any group of statesmen who take part in a political upheaval ; who uproot existing conditions and disturb settled interests ; and who bid, each after his own fashion, for popular support and approval. The chief leaders in the federation movement survived to comparatively recent years. The last of them, Sir Charles Tupper, died in the autumn of 1915. All were closely associated with party politics. There yet live many who walked and talked with them, who rejoiced with them in victory and condoled with them in defeat. It were vain to hope that the voice of faction has been silenced and that the labours of the Fathers can be viewed in the serene atmosphere which strips the mind of prejudice and passion. And yet the attempt should be made, because the founders of Canada are entitled to share the fame of those who made the nineteenth century remarkable for the unification of states and the expansion of popular government.

During Sir John Macdonald's lifetime his admirers called him the Father of Confederation. In length and prestige of official service and in talent for leadership he had no equals. His was the guiding hand after the union. The first constructive measures that cemented the Dominion are identified with his régime. When he died in the twenty-fourth year of Confederation he had been prime minister for nearly nineteen years. To his contemporaries

he towered above others. Time established
his reputation and authority. The personal
attachment of his followers was like to nothing
we have seen since, because to their natural
pride in his political triumphs was added a
passionate devotion to the man himself. His
opponents have cheerfully borne tribute to the
fascination he exercised over young and old.
Holton's delightfully ambiguous remark, on
the occasion of Macdonald's marvellous re-
storation to office in 1878, is historic : ' Well !
John A. beats the devil.' Sir Oliver Mowat
said, ' He was a genial man, a pleasant com-
panion, full of humour and wit.' Even his
satirical foe, Sir Richard Cartwright, recognized in him an unusual personality impressing
all who came in contact with it. ' He had
an immense acquaintance,' wrote Cartwright,
' with men of all sorts and conditions from one
end of Canada to the other.'

As long as he lived, therefore, an impartial
estimate of Macdonald's share in effecting Confederation could not be expected. After his
death the glamour of his name prevented a
critical survey of his achievements. Even yet
it is too soon to render a final verdict. He
took control of the situation at an early stage,
because to frame a new constitution was a task

after his own heart. He managed the Quebec Conference with the arts which none of the other members possessed in equal degree. As political complications arose his remarkable astuteness soon overcame them; and he emerged from the negotiations the most conspicuous figure in a distinguished group. It is inevitable that genius for command should overshadow the merits of others. True in every line of endeavour, this is especially so in politics. With his great gifts, Macdonald preserved his ascendancy in the young nation and was the chief architect of its fortunes for many years.

To assert, however, that one person was the author of Confederation, in the sense that the others played subordinate parts and were mere satellites revolving round the sun, is to mistake the nature and history of the movement. It was a long battle against adverse influences. If left unchallenged, they forbade the idea of a Dominion stretching from sea to sea. It was not Macdonald who forced the issue to the front, who bore down stubborn opposition, and who rallied to its support the elements indispensable to success. Into the common fund contributions were made from many sources. At least eight of the Fathers of Confederation

AN ELECTION CAMPAIGN—GEORGE BROWN ADDRESSING
AN AUDIENCE OF FARMERS

From a colour drawing by C. W. Jefferys

THE WORK OF THE FATHERS 181

must be placed in the first rank of those to whom Canada owes undying gratitude. The names of Brown, Cartier, Galt, Macdonald, Tupper, Tilley, McGee, and McDougall stand pre-eminent. All these performed services, each according to his opportunities, which history will not ignore.

The foremost champion of union at the critical moment was George Brown. But for him, it is easy to believe, Confederation might have been delayed for a generation or never have come at all. His enthusiasm inspired the willing and carried the doubting. In the somewhat rare combination of courage, force, and breadth of view no one excelled him. As a political tactician he was not so successful, and to this defect may be traced the entanglements in which he was prone to land both himself and his party. His resignation from the coalition in 1865 was a mistake. It could not be explained. In leaving the ship before it reached the haven of safety he laid himself open to charges of spleen and instability. Impulsive he was, but not unstable, and his jealousy was not greater than other men's. He was always embarrassed by the fact that the criticisms of his newspaper the *Globe*, in the exercise of its undoubted rights as an organ of public opinion, were laid at his door. He found, as other editors have found, that the compromises of political life and the freedom of the press are natural enemies. In his patriotic sacrifice in behalf of Confederation lies his best claim to the respect and affection of his countrymen.

The quality most commonly ascribed to Cartier is courage; and rightly so. But equally important were his freedom from religious bigotry and his devotion to the interests of his own people. He guarded at every step the place of his race in the constitution of the Dominion; and if we are to believe the story that he fought stoutly in London for strict adherence to every concession agreed upon at Quebec, his insight into the future proved equal to his courage. The French were rooted in the belief that union meant for them a diminished power. There were grounds for the apprehension. To Cartier was due the subordination of prejudice to the common good. He was great enough to see that if Lower Canada was to become the guardian of its special interests and privileges, Upper Canada must be given a similar security; and this threw him into the closest alliance with Brown. This principle, as embodied in the constitu-

THE WORK OF THE FATHERS 183

tion, is the real basis of Confederation, which
cannot be seriously menaced as long as neither
of the central provinces interferes with the
other. Cartier exemplified in his own person
the truth that the French are a tolerant and
kindly community, and that pride of race, displayed within its own proper bounds, makes
for the strength and not the weakness of the
Dominion. Unhappily, his health declined,
and he did not live to lead his race in the development of that larger patriotism of which,
with good reason, he believed them to be
capable. But his example survives, and its
influence will be felt in the generations to
come.

What share Galt had in affecting Cartier's
course is not fully known, but the two men
between them dominated Lower Canada, and
their *rapprochement* was more than a match for
the nullifying efforts of Dorion and Holton.
Galt's best work was also done before the con-
summation of the union. After 1867 he practically retired from the activities of politics,
owing more to a distaste for the yoke of party
than to any loss of interest in the welfare of
Canada. He had an ample mind, and in his
speeches and writings there is a valuable
legacy of suggestion.

Thomas D'Arcy McGee was the orator of the movement. While other politicians hung back, he proclaimed the advantages of union in season and out with the zeal of the crusader. His speeches, delivered in the principal cities of all the provinces, did much to rouse patriotic fervour.

To Tupper and to Tilley, as this narrative has sought to show, we owe the adherence of the Maritime Provinces. The present Dominion would have been impossible but for their labours and sacrifice. A federated state without an Atlantic seaboard would have resulted in a different destiny for Canada. Each of these statesmen withstood the temptation to bend before the storm of local prejudice. By yielding to the passion of the hour each would have been a hero in his own province and have enjoyed a long term of office. If evidence were needed that Confederation inspired its authors to nobler aims than party victories, the course taken by these leaders furnishes conclusive proof.

William McDougall's part in the movement has suffered eclipse owing to his political mishaps. No one brought more brilliant qualities to bear upon the work than he. On the platform and in parliament he had, as a

speaker, no superior. In his newspaper, the
North American, he had espoused a federal
union as the first article of his political
creed; and when Brown purchased the paper,
McDougall, as the chief writer for the *Globe*,
strengthened Brown's hands and became his
natural ally in the coalition. They quarrelled
openly when McDougall elected to cast in his
lot with Macdonald in the first Dominion
ministry. The Red River episode ruptured
his relations with Macdonald, who never again
sought his support. Avoided by both leaders
and never tolerant of party discipline, McDou-
gall sought to fill the rôle of independent critic
and thus earned for himself, unfairly, the
sobriquet ' Wandering Willie.' But the Dominion owed much to his constructive talent.
There is evidence that his influence was potent
in the constitutional conferences, and that
during his term as minister he had a strong
hand in shaping public policy.

Oliver Mowat left politics for the judicial
bench immediately after the Quebec Conference. He has related that, as the delegates
sat round the table, Macdonald, on being notified of the vacancy in the vice-chancellorship
of Upper Canada, silently passed him a note
in appreciative terms offering him the place.

For seven years he remained on the bench. But he returned in 1872 to active political life, and his services to the nation as prime minister of Ontario display his balanced judgment and clearness of intellect.

Some Canadian statesmen who were invaluable to the new nationality suffer in being judged too exclusively from a party standpoint. Canada was fortunate in drawing from the ranks of both Conservatives and Liberals many men capable of developing the Dominion and adapting an untried constitution to unforeseen conditions. None had quite the same opportunities as Sir John Macdonald, who not only helped to frame the union but administered its policy for a lengthy period. Alexander Mackenzie gave the country an example of rectitude in public life and of devotion to duty which is of supreme value to all who recognize that free government may be undermined and finally destroyed by selfishness and corruption. Edward Blake, with his lofty conceptions of national ambition and his profound insight into the working of the constitution, also exerted a beneficial effect on the evolution of the state. He, like Sir John Thompson, was a native of the country. In temperament, in breadth of mind, and in contempt for petty and sordid aims, Blake and Thompson had much in common. They, and others who are too near our own day for final judgment, fully grasped the work of the Fathers and helped to give Canada its honourable status in the British Empire and its distinctive place as a self-governing community.

A retrospective glance reveals the extent to which the Fathers attained their principal objects. A threefold purpose inspired them. Their first duty was to evolve a workable plan of government. In this they succeeded, as fifty years of experience shows. The constitution, after having stood the usual tests and strain, is firmly rooted in national approval; and this result has been reached by healthy normal processes, not by exaggerated claims or a spurious enthusiasm. The constitution has always been on trial, so to speak, because Canadians are prone to be critical of their institutions. But at every acute crisis popular discontent has been due to maladministration and not to defects of organization. The structure itself stands a monument to those who erected it.

In the second and most trying of their tasks, the unification of the provinces, the Fathers were also triumphant. From the beginning the country was well stocked with pessimists and Job's comforters. They derived inspiration during many years from the brilliant writings of Goldwin Smith. But in the end even the doubters had to succumb to the stern logic of the facts. Under any federation, growth in unity is bound to be slow. The relations of the provinces to the federal power must be worked out and their relations to each other must be adjusted. Time alone could solve such a problem. Until the system took definite shape national sentiment was feeble. But a modified and well-poised federation, with its strong central government and its carefully guarded provincial rights, at last won the day. Years of doubt and trial there were, but in due course the Nova Scotian came to regard himself as a Canadian and the British Columbian ceased to feel that a man from the East was a foreigner. The provinces have steadily developed a community of interest. They meet cordially in periodical conferences to discuss the rights and claims possessed in common, and if serious, even menacing, questions are not dealt with as they should be, the failure will be traced to faulty statesmanship and not to lack of unity.

To preserve the Imperial tie was the third and greatest object of the Fathers. They realized that many dangers threatened it—some tangible and visible, others hidden and beyond the ken of man. It may not be denied that the barque of the new nationality was launched into an unknown sea. The course might conceivably lead straight to complete independence, and honest minds, like Galt's, were held in thrall by this view. Could monarchy in any shape be re-vitalized on the continent where the Great Republic sat entrenched? What sinister ideas would not the word Imperialism convey to the practical men of the western world? These fears the Fathers met with resolute faith and the seeing eye. They believed that inherent in the beneficent rule of Queen Victoria there was a constitutional sovereignty which would appeal irresistibly to a young democracy; that unwavering fidelity to the crown could be reconciled with the fullest extension of self-government; and that the British Empire when organized on this basis would hold its daughter states beyond the seas with bonds that would not break.

And so it has proved. Of all the achievements of the Fathers this is the most splendid and enduring. The Empire came to mean, not the survival of antiquated ideas, but the blessings of a well-ordered civilization. And when in 1914 the Great War shook the world, Canadians, having found that the sway of Britain brought them peace, honour, and contentment, were proud to die for the Empire. To debate the future of Canada was long the staple subject for abstract discussion, but the march of events has carried us past the stage of idle imaginings. A knowledge of the laws by which Divine Providence controls the destinies of nations has thus far eluded the subtlest intellect, and it may be impossible for any man, however gifted, to foresee what fate may one day overtake the British Empire. But its traditions of freedom and toleration, its ideals of pure government and respect for law, can be handed on unimpaired through the ages. The opportunity to maintain and perpetuate these traditions and ideals is the priceless inheritance which Canada has received from the Fathers of Confederation.

BIBLIOGRAPHICAL NOTE

THE printed material relative to Confederation is voluminous. The earliest proposals are to be found in the *Constitutional Documents* by Shortt and Doughty. The parliamentary debates of the four provinces from 1864 to 1867 record the progress of the movement which culminated in the British North America Act. For the intimate history of the coalition ministry and the conferences in Quebec and in London the two works by Sir Joseph Pope, *Memoirs of Sir John Macdonald* and *Confederation Documents*, are mines of indispensable information. The files of the Toronto *Globe* and the Halifax *Chronicle* are valuable, while the pamphlets, especially those relating to the events in Quebec and Nova Scotia, are essential. Gray's *Confederation* confirms other material, but is not in itself of paramount importance. Mr Chisholm's *Speeches and Public Letters of Joseph Howe* and Dr Saunders's *Three Premiers of Nova Scotia* must be consulted. Mr John Boyd's *Sir George Etienne Cartier: His Life and Times* exhibits full knowledge and is free from bias. See also the *Life and Speeches of*

George Brown, by Alexander Mackenzie, which contains some valuable material. For a clear and impartial biography of Brown, see *George Brown,* by John Lewis. For the period after the union, consult Pope's *Memoirs of Sir John Macdonald* and Sir John Willison's *Sir Wilfrid Laurier and the Liberal Party.* The Life and *Times of Sir Leonard Tilley* by James Hannay and Sir Charles Tupper's *Recollections* throw light on the question in the Maritime Provinces. The official dispatches between the colonial secretary and the governors of the provinces laid before the Imperial parliament are collected in one volume. Mr William Houston's *Constitutional Documents* contains useful notes.

See also *Canada and its Provinces,* vols. v, vi, xiii, xix, xxi; and, in the present Series, *The Day of Sir John Macdonald, The Day of Sir Wilfrid Laurier,* and *The Railway Builders.*

INDEX

Printed by T. and A. Constable, Printers to His Majesty
at the Edinburgh University Press

THE CANIS[...]

BU[...]